GHOST TOWNS
OF BRITISH COLUMBIA

GHOST TOWNS

OF BRITISH COLUMBIA

By Bruce Ramsey

PUBLISHED BY
MITCHELL PRESS LIMITED
VANCOUVER, CANADA

FIRST PRINTING DECEMBER 1963
SECOND PRINTING FEBRUARY 1966
THIRD PRINTING JANUARY 1968
FOURTH PRINTING JANUARY 1970
FIFTH PRINTING DECEMBER 1971

Printed in Canada
MITCHELL PRESS LIMITED
Vancouver, B.C.

To all those who
called these deserted places
"My Home Town"

Contents

PART I

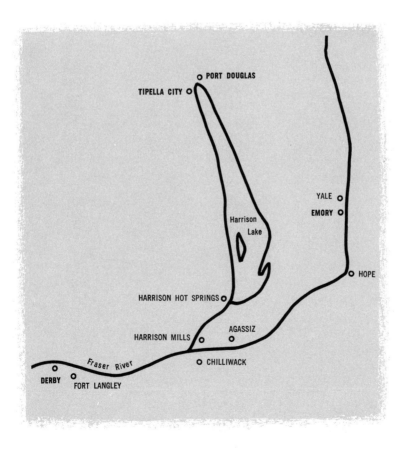

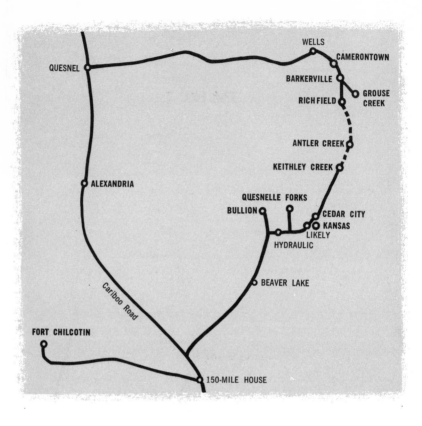

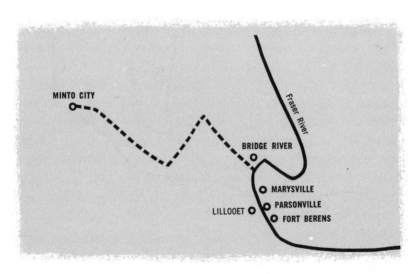

Harrison Mills in the days when the saws squealed.

Harrison Mills

AFTER TWO or three quick pulls on the lanyard the inboard motor began
to sputter and finally purred contentedly. In a few minutes, gentle little
waves began to lick the shoreline of placid Harrison Bay. The Odyssey
of the Ghost Towns was begun.

Slowly, the community of Harrison Mills faded into the background,
and the sounds of civilization—cars, trains and other human voices—grew
dimmer and only the putt-putt of the engine and the winds whispering
amongst the tall cedars and alders remained. The Harrison River, sometimes fast, but mostly rather sluggish, was becoming a place to slip the
leash on city-snarled thoughts, and to let them roam free and soar to
dazzling heights, like the eagle which seemed to follow the little boat
as it chugged northward towards Harrison Lake and the town of Port
Douglas at its upper end.

In the days when British Columbia was emerging from its role as a
Hudson's Bay Company fur preserve, gold-hungry men, fur traders,
soldiers, statesmen, fancy ladies, beggar men and thieves had passed this
way *enroute* to the diggings on the upper Fraser and in the Cariboo.

And down this river highway came shipments of gold dust and men
with stories that were to inflame the world and create the great gold
rush of the 1860s.

But now the river is lonely. Deserted farms decay in the bush along

3

its banks, and the empty windows of disintegrating buildings speak of the past, perhaps of shattered dreams, or maybe of contentment with life in the open. Who knows but they?

Everything seems to hinge on "the past", and the past comes to life in Acton Kilby's general store at Harrison Mills.

You can roam the length and breadth of British Columbia, sampling its many and varied moods, and yet, always, you feel drawn to return to Kilby's store. It evokes memories of an easier-going, more secure time when the West was filled with enterprise and an all-pervading optimism. Here, more than most places, time has stood still.

Once the Mills was an important centre, with sternwheel ferry boats shuttling up and down the Harrison, and then across the swift-flowing Fraser to landings on the Chilliwack side, connecting that rich farm area with the trans-continental railway. Once, too, the scream of saws biting into solid timbers and the hissing of steam pleasantly rent the air. But they are gone and Harrison Mills is now a gentle, rural community adjoining an Indian reserve. Thundering diesel locomotives haul a nation's produce past the sole remnant of Harrison Mills, past the high-level, stilted, false fronted, wonderful general store.

In the beginning, Kilby's store was a "temperance hotel", providing meals and rooms, as well as a store and post office for travellers from the south side of the river. The Kilbys have been there since 1904, and although there is no connection between the two, this was the year the Great Troubles began.

In the early days the Hudson's Bay Company operated a store on the site of the present Roman Catholic church on the reserve, and for many years this simple, white church was guarded by a small cannon, an historic remnant of an earlier time. The cannon now stands, unmarked, in front of a store in Hope. When the Harrison Route to the gold fields was abandoned in favor of the Cariboo Road through the Fraser Canyon, the importance of Harrison's "Bay" steadily dropped, and it eventually closed.

During the last decade of the 19th Century the Martin Brothers started a sawmill here, and this business was taken over in 1900 by the Tretheweys to become enriched with the grandiose name, Harrison Mills Timber & Trading Company. In 1904 the first of the Troubles appeared. The property was sold to Rat Portage Lumber Co., but during the transfer negotiations the mill burned down. A new plant was erected, but after two seasons' work, it was shut down, and for ten years the mill lay idle, finally being dismantled.

The next event in the fall of Harrison Mills occured in 1912 and it was as good as a *coup de grace*, for after it happened the town lost ambition. In that year railway track layers completed the lower section of the *Canadian Northern Railway* on the south side of the Fraser, so therefore, Chilliwack residents no longer had to cross the river by steamboat to Harrison Mills to get a train for Vancouver or

Another satisfied customer at Kilby's general store.

New Westminster. Three years later the *CNR* spanned the continent and Harrison Mills was finished. It had lost it prime reasons for being.

Business on the steamboats fell to practically nothing, and it is said that Capt. R. C. Menten, of the *Minto*, used to flip a coin with the chief engineer as to who would get the proceeds for the day. At the mouth of the Harrison, at low water, the wreck of another Harrison River boat, the *J. P. Douglas*, can be seen.

But, wonderfully, Acton Kilby's store remains, a strong hold-out for the past, and probably the last fortress in B.C. against the loudly-touted soft detergents which, it is said, make dish washing easy and a pleasure.

"We carry two kinds of soap powder," Mr. Kilby tells his customers, "white and blue. One dollar for a five-pound bag of the white and $1.25 for the blue."

Eggs are sold, not in the conventional carton, but wrapped individually in newspapers and stuffed into empty soft drink cartons which the customers bring. Candy is displayed in great elongated glass bottles, as are dried peas, beans and other soup-making staples. Hardware items of many and varied sorts, both old-fashioned and modern, hang from the ceiling, and there is hardly an inch of free space in the whole establishment.

Age and the elements have weathered this store, but on the other hand, time seems to have passed it by, leaving this, the first ghost town on our itinerary, one to be long remembered in an era when the super markets tend to make us forget the little general stores of our fathers.

An old engraving of Port Douglas.

Port Douglas

IT MUST BE recorded that our inboard motorboat never reached Harrison Lake, nor the town of Port Douglas at its head. This had to wait for a later day and a surer and safer form of transportation, as Harrison Lake, without notice, can suddenly become a most unpleasant stretch of water.

But the spirit of Port Douglas, dead for nearly a century, continued to call long after our trip up the Harrison was abandoned. We knew before we set out that there was little to touch, or to see, in the town, yet we suspected that you could still feel something of its past without actually seeing or touching anything.

At first sight, our advance impressions of Port Douglas were jolted. Down by the waterfront stands a ramshackle, balconied building looking as though it stepped out of a TV western and was out-gunned. This was exactly the type of building we wanted to find, but it was too good to be true, and we hardly dared to make enquiries fearing our dream would be punctured. Alas, it was. It was only a comparatively young abandoned boarding house, once used by a logging company.

But by merely stepping back onto the dusty road to admire this rustic bit of yesteryear, we were stepping back a hundred years or more and joining with the shades of thousands of prospectors, packers, mule skinners, even camel drivers, saints and sinners, in their march up the long and winding trail to the Cariboo. This road, which now bears the heavy weight of logging trucks, is the one thing Port Douglas clings to out of its past.

In July 1858 James Douglas, who in a few months time was to be sworn in as governor of the new Crown Colony of British Columbia, was faced with the problem of providing access to the upper Fraser River where rich placer gold ground had been found. The route through the Fraser Canyon, considering his small, or what is more correct to say, negligible treasury, was impossible to consider as a place to build a trail. But he thought back to his Hudson's Bay Company days and to a pathfinding expedition of Alexander Caulfield Anderson some ten years before.

Anderson had been seeking a route to the sea for the fur brigades from Fort St. James, far to the north, and one part of his journey had been down the Fraser to present-day Lillooet, then via a chain of lakes—which he called Seton and Anderson—the Birkenhead River, Lillooet Lake, and thence via the Harrison to the Fraser. In the end another route for the brigades was adopted, but now Douglas recalled the Harrison and saw in it the answer to his particular problem.

The Fraser, as it always does in the months of June, July and August, was running swift and high, and for this reason, mining along its banks was impossible. Some of the miners loafed and brooded about their ill-luck, and some wrote nasty letters to the editors of the San Francisco papers, others drank and gambled in Victoria's many prosperous saloons. So Douglas called a meeting of the miners, and the result was probably one of the most unique construction contracts ever offered and accepted.

The men, about 500 in number, were to be divided into 20 companies of 25 men each and would be transported to the head of Harrison Lake, free of charge, to build a trail from that point to Cayoosh, now known as Lillooet. They would receive free room and board, but no pay, and they had to put up a bond of $25 to guarantee they lived up to the agreement. This sum was to be repaid when the work was finished, not in cash, but in goods at Victoria prices.

The project began on August 5, 1858 when the steamer *Otter* left

Port Douglas today.

Victoria, and by the end of September the trail was finished. In time, steamers were placed in service on the connecting lakes, and even a horse-drawn "railroad" was operated to portage between Anderson and Seton Lakes.

The following year, members of the Royal Engineers, sent out from England to engage in public works projects, widened the trail, and until the completion of the Cariboo Road through the Canyon, which linked with the trail at Clinton, it was the "easy and elegant" way to reach the goldfields. A hundred years later much of the route is still in use, and several of the original roadhouses established to cater to the comforts of the argonauts of '58 remain, and are in remarkably good condition, though, of course, they no longer serve their first purpose.

By December of its beginning year of life, Port Douglas had about 50 houses, built of logs and shingles, and was growing fast. In February 1859 the Victoria *Gazette* reported that the town had three stores, two restaurants, two boarding houses, and "many places selling the odd thing including liquor to the Indians." There was a blacksmith, a gunsmith, bakers, cobblers, tailors, a shingle maker, carpenters, a boat builder, plus "gambling in a small way".

By March of the following year, 1859, the Royal Engineers had laid out a townsite, consisting of lots 60x120 feet. A scramble for real estate ensued, and it was charged that six people owned most of the waterfront.

Perhaps it is nothing to boast about, but Port Douglas, so it is said, witnessed the first hanging on the mainland of British Columbia. It took place December 6, 1859 when an Indian named Wichtakuch went to his doom at the end of a rope for stabbing a "Boston man", as Americans were called in the Chinook jargon. For a couple of days before the event, tension mounted as it was feared the Indians, who numbered about 700, might descend on the town and with a whoop and a holler liberate the prisoner from the little log jailhouse. Luckily, this never happened and Wichtakuch's demise was carried out without undue delay.

In its halcyon days there were five hotels, including the Douglas, which boasted a dining room 66 feet long, and accommodation for 100. There was culture, too, of a sort, in the form of the Ancient and Honourable Order of E Clampus Vitus, a name, which, even with a pile of Latin dictionaries in front of you, cannot be translated. The best we can do is take a literal crack at the meaning and call it an honourable lively stomping society, and tip our hat to the unknown Latin scholar who created new words for an ancient language on this the frontier of North America.

While not E Clampus Vitusing there was always fun in going down to the old corral and watching the reaction of the mules and horses to the camels which had been brought in by Frank Laumeister for service on the trail. Poor Frank! His idea was a good one, but in theory only. They could carry a thousand pounds of freight each, and with the existing exorbitant freight rates should have piled up a fortune for the owners. But, it is said, mules, horses, and oxen were terrified at the sight—and smell—of these "ships of the desert". The rough terrain played havoc with their hoofs, and so, Laumeister was forced to pull the unwieldy beasts from service.

With the completion, in 1864, of the canyon road, Port Douglas fell upon bad times. By May of 1866 the white population had been reduced to 24, and many of these could not be called permanent settlers. There was no business and even the Indians had no money. In October 1866 the last advertisement for a hotel at Douglas disappeared from the Victoria newspapers.

During the '90s a sawmill was in operation at the old Port, and from time-to-time railway promoters mentioned it as part of fantastic schemes to reach the Yukon and Klondyke with a ribbon of steel. It was only talk. Port Douglas' days were over.

There is, however, one continuing link with the old town, and this will be found in the City of Chilliwack. Beside the pulpit in St. Thomas' Anglican church there is a little brass plaque which states it rests on a panel from the original pulpit of St. Mark's, Port Douglas. This church was consecrated in May 1862 and early pictures of the town show it standing out above a cluster of business houses, which, the Bishop deplored, were open even on Sundays.

For three-quarters of a decade after the fall from glory of Port Douglas, the church was empty. In 1873 it was dismantled and floated down the Harrison in six Indian canoes and erected at the Five Corners, the hub of Chilliwack's business district today. The name was then changed to St. Thomas's and until 1897, when it was replaced by the present church, it served the people of the Sumas district well. In 1909 the building was removed to the present site.

Of the visible remains of Douglas, only this bit of wood, a great iron stove in the Clinton Museum, and a few artifacts in other museums remain, but the spiritual side of Port Douglas lives on in the parish of St. Thomas, Chilliwack.

Tipella City

MAPS AND DIRECTORIES of the turn of the century list a place called Tipella, sometimes with the handsome addition of City tacked to the name, as existing about three miles south-west of old Port Douglas.

From what we could learn, it was a townsite owned by the Fire Mountain Gold Mining Company which had an operation about 15 miles away up on Fire Mountain. As the B.C. *Mining Record* stated in 1898, the mine commenced operation the year before and its owners were "confident that they had the best mine in B.C."

The actual property was optimistically called the "Money Spinner" and the quartz ledge being developed stood out from the side of the mountain like a white monument, visible from the Douglas trail, and yet, as far as is known, it was not examined until the fall of 1897. At this time a mild rush was started, and one report has it that several thousand came in, but this seems somewhat of an exaggeration.

By October of '98, the *Mining Record* said, everyone in this district was waiting for the first clean-up in the Fire Mountain mine to enable them to realize "in many cases very high prices for their prospects." And when the clean-up did not come up to their hopes, most of them left for the Klondike.

Following this set-back, Tipella City declined, if in fact, it ever had boomed. But it hung on for several more years as the headquarters for the Brooks-Scanlon Lumber Company, who were listed there in the 1910 *B.C. Directory*.

One day after work a group of us were sitting around a table enjoying a mild libation, and somehow the conversation got around to the subject of Harrison Lake, probably in reference to the Sasquatch, the hairy giants of the Harrison country, who were in the news at that time. Mike Lothian, the press room foreman at the Vancouver *Province*, held his glass firmly in his hand, and solemnly said, "I'll bet you fellas have never been to Tipella City?"

Mike had lived in Tipella, but you couldn't draw him out as to what exactly Tipella City was like, no matter how hard you tried. In fact we have been able to find only one description of the "city" and we hope Mike will forgive us for putting it down in black and white. But, it seems, Tipella City consisted of only a bunkhouse, a storage shed and stables for the horses.

This description is from a story which appeared in the *Province* on November 15, 1941 by Frank Gomery. It related a tale passed down by Harry M. Keefer who had been engineer on a little ship called the *City of Tipella*, owned by the Fire Mountain mining people. It concerns a Mr. Purcell, an Englishman, who had married an Indian woman and settled down to farm at Port Douglas.

"Although Mr. Purcell prospered," Mr. Gomery wrote, "and had a large bank account at New Westminster, he feared the possibility of his family reverting to Indian. So he announced that if his daughter married an Indian she would get nothing, but if she married a white man there was $10,000 for her dowry."

A man named Morris, employed as a painter by the Harrison Hot Springs Hotel, heard about this, got gloriously drunk at the prospect and

11

offered to charter the *City of Tipella* for an immediate trip up the lake for $50. While Captain Watts was considering this offer, a Jew, who ran a second hand shop in New Westminster, appeared on the scene and made a similar offer. With the wisdom of Solomon and the chance of making a hundred bucks, Captain Watts placed one suitor in the bow and the other in the stern, and neither was told of the other's presence.

"However," Mr. Gomery's story continued, "just before arriving at Tipella both men found out. The captain and engineer Keefer had their own ideas of the fitness of things though, so, as Keefer related: 'We quietly told the Jew to take the dinghy we carried and row over to Port Douglas and arrive first.'

"The other charterer, now sobering but rather fighting mad, ran to Captain Watts to tell him somebody was stealing his boat. He also demanded that the ship try to find a way through the log jam and get him to Port Douglas.

"The Captain asked if steam was up and ordered the engine started, at the same time telling me on the quiet that something must happen to the works enroute. This was easily arranged, and we stuttered and drifted aimlessly half way across.

"Although the Jew arrived first, our boat was sighted and nothing happened until we arrived. It just happened that there was at Port Douglas a priest, either French or Italian, who, with Mr. Purcell, took the situation in hand and withheld judgment until next morning.

"It was to be a big night at Port Douglas, owing to the missionary's visit, and all the Indians for miles around had been summoned to witness his magic lantern display. When I went in, the building was in complete darkness and the smell of fish, smoke and 200 steaming Indians was terrible.

"Following a few mildly attractive religious slides came many terrifying coloured pictures of life in hell. Hints were interspersed bearing on the future of such of the grunting audience as failed to be good Indians.

"Next morning there was celebrated the wedding of Miss Purcell and the Hebrew and the dowry was paid in full. The decision was purely with the lady's future in mind, and the settled businessman was favoured against the apparently unsettled artisan."

Anyway, Mike, even though Tipella City may not have amounted to much, it did produce a quaint love story. Whether or not the newly-weds of long ago lived happily ever after, who knows?

The Rev. W. B. Crickmer preaching from a barrel to the multitude at Derby in 1859. Mr. Crickmer, who made this sketch, was rector here in 1859.

Old Fort Langley and Derby

ONE OF THE NICEST things about sitting besides a swiftly-flowing silent stream is that it is conducive to day-dreaming. And if you want to dream of adventure and far away places, we can think of no better place to go than to the banks of the Fraser, to be exact, about three miles below Fort Langley. Here stood the first Fort Langley, and here also was Derby, sometimes called New Fort Langley, which came within a hairsbreadth of becoming the capital city of British Columbia. Perhaps no other bit of ground in the Fraser Valley has seen so much excitement as have the green fields surrounding the B.C. Government Travel Bureau's stone marker.

There is precious little left to see in the form of visible relics of the past, but it is not too difficult to fall under the spell of its adventure-some past; to see the little schooner *Cadboro* sailing against the swift,

13

uncharted waters of the Fraser, making her way upstream on that pleasant day in July, 1827 to land a party of French-Canadian voyageurs and Hudson's Bay Company traders to found the Fort.

For several months the *Cadboro* remained in front of the place where we, more than a hundred years later, sat, and the crew kept a watchful eye for any Indian disturbances while the men ashore erected a fort with wooden palisades and bastions. Fort Langley was more than just a trading post, the first on the coast north of the Columbia River. It was a deliberate move to anchor the British claim to the territory, then known generally as the Oregon Country, and until the erection of Fort Victoria in 1843 it was the chief depot on the coast of what is now British Columbia. And here began British Columbia's primary industries, fishing and lumbering. That distinction is the real monument to old Fort Langley, not just the bronze plaque by the side of the road.

The year after Fort Langley was founded, the post was visited by Sir George Simpson, governor of Rupert's Land and head of the Hudson's Bay Company on this continent. One of those who accompanied him on his journey was Archibald McDonald, who remained as Factor at Fort Langley. McDonald set down in his journal a description of the Fort which appears in one of the rarest of books dealing with B.C. entitled *Peace River. A Canoe Voyage from Hudson's Bay to the Pacific* published in Toronto in 1872.

"The Fort," McDonald wrote, "is 135 feet by 120, with two good bastions, and a gallery of four feet width all around. A building (*blank in MS*) feet long, of three compartments for the men, a small log house of two compartments, in which the gentlemen themselves reside and a store (*blank in MS*) feet are now occupied, besides which there are two other buildings, one a good dwelling house, with an excellent cellar and a spacious garret, a couple of well finished chimneys are up, and the whole inside now ready for wainscotting [wooden panelling] and partitioning, four large windows in front, one in each end, and one with a corresponding door in the back. The other is a low building with only two square rooms and a fire place in each and a kitchen adjoining made of slab. The out door consists of three fields, each planted with thirty bushels of potatoes and look well. The provision shed, exclusive of table stores, is furnished with three thousand dried salmon, sixteen tierces [casks] salted ditto, thirty-six cwt flour, two cwt grease and thirty bushels of salt."

After his appointment to the Fort, McDonald sent for his young son and the lonely establishment was rocked with the childish laughter of young Ranald, the pride of his father's eye. And this lad, aged five, was to carve out a career for himself, the likes of which you read about only in adventure magazines. In fact, one bookshop which handled his biography in the 1940s went so far as to cast doubt about the authenticity of the narrative, probably not realizing that very often truth is stranger than fiction.

After young McDonald received his education he shipped off to sea and saw service on a treasure ship, a slaver—whose crew threw the human cargo overboard on the approach of a British warship—and on a whaling vessel, and it was from this enterprise that he entered into the most fantastic episode in his life. In 1848 he had himself deliberately cast ashore in forbidden Japan, and for ten months he was kept in custody, but was well treated. For seven months of this time he conducted classes in English for a group of 14 young students, several of whom acted as interpreters during the negotiations between the Japanese authorities and Commodore Perry in 1854. In the spring of 1849 he was released and set out on another adventurous road, this time to the gold rush in Australia. Finally, he returned to the banks of the Fraser to join in the gold rush to the Cariboo. For a time he operated a store at Port Douglas and a ferry across the Fraser at Lillooet, and for the next 20 years mined in the Cariboo. He died in 1894 at Fort Colvile, Washington.

There was plenty of excitement in the Fort, too, during those early days when Ranald McDonald was growing up. There was Indian warfare close by the gates, and on one occasion the guns of the bastion rained death and destruction upon a party of warlike Yucultas from the north. And, of course, there were the fur brigades bringing in the trading goods from Fort Vancouver on the lower Columbia, and with them came news from the outside.

But, sitting beside the river today and day-dreaming of the past, one only touches the dramatic high points of history, and we tend to forget the monotony, the loneliness and the hardships these fur traders endured. Only when we read the day-by-day matter of fact journals they kept can we really realize their arduous existence. At some posts the writers of the daily journal could talk of the idleness that was their lot, but Langley was busy. In its first ten years it collected a total of 14,651 beaver skins, of which no less than 10,330 were prime pelts, and in a letter to Simpson,

15

The site of old Derby. Mound in centre is all that remains of one of Royal Engineers' barracks. In background, the Houston home.

McDonald referred to the salmon catch "from the 20th of August [1830] to the 13th of the next month we were fortunate enough to procure upwards of 15,000; enough to make up more than 200 Barrels, which in that very short space we contrived to do, into nearly that number of casks of our own making, with means so imperfect, however, that I fear from the sample that remained with ourselves, the first Cargo will not stand the Test of a foreign market, and trust by the next Season, we shall be provided with a good Cooper, that will know something of fish curing."

The location had its drawbacks, and these were constantly being referred to in dispatches to the Chief Factor and to the Governor. For one thing, it was too far from the mouth of the river and ships often had great difficulty finding the channel, and, too, the area available for agriculture was too far from the Fort.

Under James Murray Yale, who succeeded McDonald, a new location was selected, and Chief Factor James Douglas, writing to London in June 1839, states "We have abandoned the old Langley establishment which was in a dilapidated state, as well as inconvenient in some respects for the business, and removed all the effects into a new fort built a few miles further up the banks of Fraser's River . . . It is fully as convenient for the fur and salmon trade as the former site. Moreover it possessed the important and desirable advantage of being much nearer the farm."

And thus, the first phase of this little plot of land passed into history, and the years rolled on, and the site, as far as recorded history is concerned, was forgotten. In 1858, while the whole lower Fraser was in the throes of a great gold rush, Douglas, now governor of British Columbia, remembered, and selected the site for a town.

"The townsite," wrote Howay and Scholefield in their monumental history of the province, "consisted of 183 blocks, each 5 to 10 chains, containing 18 lots, 64 x 120 feet. The streets, which were all unnamed, were 78 feet in width, with an alley-way of 12 feet in width through each block. The reserve price on a full-sized lot was $100. After a number of adjournments the sale was held in Victoria on the 25th, 26th and 29th of November, P.M. Backus acting as auctioneer. Three hundred and forty-three lots were disposed of, aggregating $66,172.50 . . . "

On December 1, the governor called for tenders for the erection of a church, parsonage, courthouse and jail in the new town. And it was here that the first of the Royal Engineers, under Capt. J. M. Grant and Capt. R. M. Parsons, established their headquarters and began the erection of barrack buildings to be ready for the main force to arrive early the next year in the *Thames City*.

Douglas said his selection was guided by the "partiality displayed for this site by the mercantile community of the country [meaning, of course, the Hudson's Bay Company] whose instincts on such matters are generally unerring."

Perhaps this was so in the selection of trading posts, but not for townsites. At high water, most of Derby was under water, and, as Colonel R. C. Moody, of the Royal Engineers, remarked on his arrival, "Everything is against it, the river is not deep enough for sea going vessels; it is in a low position and on the wrong side of the river for defensive purposes."

The famous Judge Begbie remarked that "this place has a desolate look . . . water is all over the centre of town."

Douglas bowed to Moody and a new site was chosen. New Westminster was born. However, before this was done, the Church of St. John

A sketch by the Rev. W. B. Crickmer, 1859.

and adjacent rectory were built and the Rev. W. B. Crickmer was appointed rector. In his memoirs Mr. Crickmer tells us the church was of his own design: "the cloth for the Communion table I compounded of the red cloth and lace tassels traded by the Hudson's Bay Company to the Indians for salmon, as also the desk and pulpit cloths."

By May 1 the church was finished, and the first service held. Seven months later, on January 8, 1860 the final entry in the register was made.

Mr. Crickmer was a remarkable man, and much good can be said of his work in the mining camps of the lower Fraser. In addition to his religious work, Mr. Crickmer was a bit of an artist, and his drawings are the only pictorial records we have of what Derby looked like. He sketched himself standing on a barrel preaching in the main street; he pictured the church and the rectory and himself doing the household chores. Without these sketches, our day-dreaming would be much more difficult!

Today all that remains of Derby are the barest outlines of the barrack buildings built by the Royal Engineers, and the church, but this building is no longer on the original site. For 20 years it was used occasionally by Presbyterians and Methodists, and in 1881 a group of Anglicans moved it to Maple Ridge where it stands today on the corner of River Road and Third Avenue, the sole remaining building of old Derby.

There is, however, one more chapter to be written in the annals of this bit of historic ground. After the townsite was abandoned, the land was taken up by a soldier of fortune by the name of James Houston, whose descendants occupy the land to this day. It was this James Houston who, in 1856, discovered gold at Tranquille Creek, near Kamloops, and it was this discovery which led to the first rush of miners to the Thompson River. It was a party of miners, bound for this new field, who found gold just below Yale . . .

Yes, at old Fort Langley, Derby and the Houston farm, there's many a ghost of the past. Day-dreaming there is remarkably easy, and very, very pleasant.

The old church of St. John the Divine at its present location in Maple Ridge. It is the oldest church in British Columbia.

19

Street scene at Emory City during construction of the Canadian Pacific Railway.

Emory City

LITTLE CHILDREN now scamper along what was once the main street of Emory City, and they play, without realizing it, amongst the foundations of the saloons, hotels and restaurants, which, for a few short years back in the early 1880s, made up a town that lived as few other towns did. It was fated, like so many others, to die and be forgotten.

The "City" is now a provincial government picnic site, four miles south of Yale. Its geographic position has been given as being "Below Hell's Gate and Beyond Hope", and perhaps, when you come right down to it, that description pretty well fills the bill.

It was here that Andrew Onderdonk's contract for the construction of the *Canadian Pacific Railway* through the Fraser and Thompson River canyons to Savona began. And as a result, Emory City came into being.

Two decades before Onderdonk began his task of quarrying the railway grade out of the formidable cliffs of the canyon, Emory was already in the news.

On February 12, 1859 "W.H.D." told the Victoria *Colonist* that he was "sinking 2 shafts down to the pay gravel from 400 to 450 feet back from the river and from these prospects we expect to make from half to an ounce a day to the hand."

Exactly a month later the *Colonist* reported "the country below Fort Yale is fast being deserted. The miners are all going above. At Emory's Bar where nearly 500 men lived during the winter, there are scarcely thirty—all gone up-river. Those who remain are doing tolerably well." Within a month, though, Emory was again booming, for on April 9 we read: "Emory Bar which was nearly deserted recently is again being worked by newcomers, most of whom affirm that they make from 8 to 12 dollars per day with rockers. Another stratum of pay dirt has been struck about three feet below the one just worked out."

And so it went. Wave after wave of miners striking the Fraser, reworking old claims and then moving on. By March 13, 1860 it was anticipated that, come July, Emory Bar would be deserted again as the miners were "pushing towards Quesnelle River, but another influx of strangers was expected to the deserted bars."

Mining, it seems from a story in the *Colonist* of August 8, 1859, was not the only activity carried on at Emory Bar. The law swooped down one day and "two men, heretofore enjoying good reputations, were brought up from Emory Bar [to Yale] . . . on a charge of supplying fire water to the poor natives and being convicted were fined £12 each." The report also noted that "two women (!)" on the same bar were fined £5 and that 17 gallons "of a villainous compound which it would be a libel on whisky to call by that name, was seized by the officer in one of the houses searched."

When the bar at the mouth of the creek which flows through the present-day picnic ground was finally deserted, the property passed into the hands of a man named Walker who, the *Inland Sentinel*, later published at Emory City, said "secured this place at an early day and hung on for years, expecting that it would eventually become the head of navigation. He finally lost confidence and went 'where the woodbine twineth' or somewhere else." He apparently sold out early in 1879, and how he must have cursed his luck, because in the October 7, 1879 issue of the *Colonist* there is this paragraph:

"FORTUNATE SPECTATORS: The entire townsite of Emory Bar, the temporary terminus of the CPR and the future head of steamboat navigation on Fraser River, is owned by the Oppenheimer Bros. who bought it last spring for a song."

The Oppenheimers were the leading merchants of their day in B.C., and one of them, David, was to be a member of the first city council of Vancouver and that metropolis' second mayor. It did not take them very long to convert Emory Bar into Emory City, for on February 3, 1880 the *Colonist* announced that the sale of town lots was fixed for March 1. On the day following the epic announcement, details of the ambitious city were announced:

"Emory City has 13 streets and is divided into 32 blocks which contain 400 lots of goodly dimensions. The streets that run parallel with the river are named Front, First, Second, Third, Fourth and Fifth; those running at right angles to the river are named King, Queen, Princess, Argyll, Lisgar, Elgin and Pacific. Through the centre of the town runs Emory Creek, from which an illimitable supply of our mountain water will be had, and the front of the town is laved by the Mighty Fraser."

When the lots came up for auction, according to the March 17 *Colonist* "the competition for several of the most eligibly situated lots was especially lively and at the fall of the hammer Mr. L. Lowenberg, representing foreign capital, was declared the purchaser." The highest price paid for any lot was $550, with the average being about $250. The sale, especially the purchases by "foreign capital", the paper noted, "demonstrates a confidence in the future of Emory City which is thoroughly justifiable. It would be no matter of surprise to learn within the course of a few months that any one of the lucky speculators yesterday had bought himself suddenly rich."

And then the boom began. On March 25, 1880 the first batch of workmen arrived in New Westminster and proceeded up-river to Emory and Yale. This group consisted of 204 white men and 31 Chinese. A few days later, the *Dominion Pacific Herald* at New Westminster reported, "Of Onderdonk's 'Frisco boys who went up to Yale last week, 12 were in the lock-up the first night and 20 the second." These were "Onderdonk's Lambs", the motley crew who were to forge the steel rail link between Atlantic and Pacific and make the dream of Canadian Confederation a reality.

In May, Captain John Irving's *Pioneer Steamboats* were making Emory City a port of call, and the principal streets were being laid out and graded. Michael Hagen was erecting a two-storey building for his *Inland Sentinel*, and Gray & Hay's steam sawmill was under construction.

At 11 o'clock on the morning of May 14, 1880 the first shot of dynamite was fired on construction, with the Montreal *Gazette* reporting that "Mr. Onderdonk at the request of the Hon. J. W. Trutch, ordered the foreman to light the fuse—a grand success; the loud noise resounded in the Fraser Valley some distance, besides causing a down-pour of rain."

Hagen's *Inland Sentinel* began publishing at Emory in May 1880, with 99 percent of the advertisements coming from the merchants of Yale. Judging from the pen-sketch of Emory, there was not much to draw advertising from, as saloons did not need to advertise their wares to Onderdonk's Lambs. On pay day the bars would be jammed, and a description given to Yale on pay day would apply equally to Emory: "Bizarre, risque and grotesque."

"We are upon the eve of another Railway payday," said the *Sentinel* of February 3, 1881, "and we would remind those of the workmen who work hard from month to month and come to town for their pay, where they too often remain upon "the spree" until the last dollar is spent, that doubtless, poor Cronan's life was sacrificed by such a course. When the money is gone they have no longer "friends" and the jail is generally the resort.

"Those with robust constitutions may stand it for a time, but such abuse will undermine health and leave disease and want in the train. Once the money is squandered very little care need be expected, and, as in the case mentioned, a premature death is the result. After a hurried inquiry as to the cause, the remains are hurried away in a rough coffin—

> 'Rattle his bones over the stones
> He is a pauper nobody owns'

—and dumped in a hole in the ground. Let those unfortunately addicted to strong drink take heed; it is difficult to say who the next victim will be."

The lecture on sobriety fell on deaf ears. But if you wanted to improve your health the bar keeper could supply you with Ayers Sarsaparilla "for purifying the blood."

Hagen tried his best to boost Emory City, but his best was not good enough. In August, 1880 he wrote: "Emory is now fairly upon the highway to be something more than a city in name. It only requires time to give this beautiful location . . . a business importance that must lead to a large and prosperous population." But in October the cold hard facts of reality showed themselves and on the 21st Hagen moved the

23

paper to Yale, hoping to move back in the spring if business should look up. But business didn't.

Although the *Inland Sentinel* stayed only a brief time in Emory City, it did provide a link between the earliest days of news-papering in British Columbia and the present. The press he used was the first to come to Victoria, having been brought in by the Right Rev. Modeste Demers, first Roman Catholic bishop of Victoria, in 1852. It does not seem to have been used until 1858 when, in September of that year, Paul de Garro printed the first newspaper in that city, a French-language journal entitled *Le Courier de la Nouvelle Caledonie*. Shortly afterwards de Garro printed Alfred Waddington's little book *Fraser River Mines Vindicated*, on it. This was the first book published on Vancouver Island. And, in November of that momentous year of 1858, Amor de Cosmos used it to print the first issues of the *Colonist*. In 1865 it was hauled up the Cariboo Road and used to print the *Cariboo Sentinel* at Barkerville. And then this little press, now a treasured possession of St. Ann's Convent in Victoria, came to Emory City. From here it went to Yale, and, with Hagen a few years later, went up to Kamloops. In the passage of time, this paper, started in Emory City, became the Kamloops *Sentinel*.

Apparently, after the initial sale of town lots, real estate values did not go up as anticipated. For nearly a year, from the summer of 1881 to the end of June 1882, lots were offered at private sales "at an upset price," and one of those who was unloading was the dapper "Baron" of Victoria, Leopold Lowenberg who had represented "foreign capital" at the initial sale.

But even though the *Sentinel* had deserted Emory for the plush advertising revenues of Yale, the little "city" continued to function. On May 11, 1881, the first locomotive ever seen in British Columbia was unloaded from a river steamer and placed on the tracks. With a journalist's trained eye, Hagen looked at the iron monster and noted in his paper that "the engine is evidently a good one."

Early in June the engine reached Yale itself. "An impromptu committee of Messrs. Mitchell, Leiser and McPhee soon waited upon a few of our inhabitants and raised 'the needful.' Powder and a barrel of beer were procured and the Engine, with a shrill whistle announcing its presence at 6 p.m., the 'little giant' cannon roared out a salute in response. Messrs. Ash, Corbett, Fisher and Carry, gunners, while the workmen under Mr. Munro slaked their thirst in the foaming beverages . . . After a brief stay the Engine and four cars with three lorries left with the 30 odd workmen for their headquarters at Emory."

The big show, and as far as news reports went, the finale, for Emory City, was on the Fourth of July 1881, when a popular pastime, one which was to last for decades to come, the railway excursion, was introduced to British Columbia.

To prepare for the event, a special run was made by the sternwheeler *William Irving* from New Westminster. She arrived in Yale the night before, bedecked in flags, an array which contained the tattered colours flown from her predecessors on the river, such famed ships as the *Onward*, *Lillooet*, *Reliance* and *Glenora*.

Everybody was in a holiday mood, and at Emory the excursionists were promised meals at either of the two hotels, the American and the Emory, at 50 cents each, racing, quoit pitching and swings for the ladies. Tickets were sold at 50 cents with the proceeds going to the Fire Company funds.

The New Westminster brass band was on hand, and when the puffing steam engine slowly pulled away from Yale's station, it struck up "Hail, Columbia" and for the four-mile trip the air was literally rent with oompah music. Arriving at Emory City, the engine promptly turned around and went back to Yale to pick up another load.

"Soon the Excursionists were sightseeing in the embryo city," the *Sentinel* said, "the Band remaining near the hotel where the dancing platform had been erected under cover, the necessary music was provided and the tripping upon light fantastic toes commenced in earnest, the ladies especially evidently enjoying the exercise . . . For a time others of the Excursionists visited the Emory Hotel and scattered around the scenery."

The day ended with a horse race along Front Street, and a nag from Hope won, and then the crowd piled back on the train for the return trip to Yale. Emory City had never seen such a day, and although it was a favourite picnic site for the people of Yale, its moment of glory was gone. Two "firsts" were enough.

After that Emory City became the supply base for construction. All supplies for the camps strung along the line as far up as Savona were unloaded here. With the completion of the line in 1885, the town was deserted as rapidly as it arose.

And so, for the obituary of Emory City, let us read from the *B.C. Directory* for 1885:

"The railway warehouses are located here and it is the first station that has the appearance of a town after leaving Port Haney for Yale. The town of Emory possesses excellent hotels, general stores, etc."

In other words, Emory City "died with a good press."

Parsonville, Marysville, Fort Berens, Bridge River, and Minto City

DRIVING OUT from Lytton, at the junction of the Fraser and the Thompson, and up the winding and dusty road to Lillooet, 50 miles Northwest, we had to keep the obvious question "why bother?" out of our minds. And curiously, in so doing, we convinced ourselves that there was good and sufficient reason for bothering, although we well knew that no traces of Parsonville, Marysville, or Fort Berens, opposite Lillooet, could be found. And the same applied for the short-lived "town" at Bridge River and Minto City in the hills far behind.

The existence of the three places opposite Lillooet had been drawn to our attention by Artie Phair, a gentle little man, long in years, but short in signs of showing it. Ambiguously, Artie pointed across the river from his cabin in Lillooet and stated, "There was Fort Berens, there was Parsonville, and there was Marysville!" In his mind's eye, all these places were there, but the only identifiable landmark we could ascertain was a gash in the river bank, near the pumping station for the B.C. Hydro experimental farm. That was Parsonville.

According to the *Colonist* for January 12, 1863, this was Parsonville:

"Parsonville is situated on the west bank of the Fraser opposite Lillooet, and when a bridge is placed over the river, will form a part of the same town. At present there are few houses erected, but like its neighbours on the other side of the water, it has progressive tendencies. It

26

contains a fine hotel conducted by Messrs. Crawford & Mathewson, and has a number of stores and saloons. In summer it is made the headquarters by packers coming down for goods and is a lively place. A number of Indians are located around and seem to get a good living by honest industry."

Marysville, probably smaller than Parsonville, was upstream a few hundred yards, judging from Artie's directions, and Fort Berens, built in 1859 by the Hudson's Bay Company, occupied a point on a bench above where the Fraser makes a great turn, about a hundred yards or so below Parsonville.

Little is recorded concerning Marysville, and Fort Berens had small chance to win notoriety. The Fort was a dependency of Fort Kamloops and was probably intended more as a fisheries post than a trading centre. Work on the buildings was started in February, 1859 but on July 4 word was received at Kamloops "to stop all work at Fort Berens and on no account to incur any further expense there and that all the tools, etc., etc. of the HBC's to be brought to Kamloops." Three days later these instructions were sent to Fort Berens and by August 25th the demolition was complete.

Bridge River, on the other hand, received quite a bit of publicity in May of 1859, as recorded in the Victoria *Gazette* for the 28th: "This little town, situated about three hundred yards above the mouth of Bridge River, consists of four stores, one restaurant, a bakery, one blacksmith shop and several tents of parties located temporarily in this locality. Directly in front, a neat and commodious toll bridge, 100-feet long, 8½ feet wide and ten feet above the high water mark, has been constructed at a cost exceeding $1450. A majority of the miners in the neighborhood congregate here on Saturday and Sunday of each week to lay in their supplies, get express matter, discuss the news"; and it was here that "our special travelling correspondent heard rumours of rich gold discoveries above Fort Alexandria."

Thus, from this now deserted spot, came the first news of the great Cariboo placer fields along the Quesnel River.

In May of 1859 a company of Chinese was camped "in town" making rockers to work claims farther up the river, and a clash between the Celestials and the Indians was described by the correspondent to the *Gazette*: (Rare, indeed, was the news writer of those days who called a Chinese anything but a Celestial.)

"During their stay the Indians had been somewhat insolent to them, and some drunken white brute had encouraged one Indian to such an extent that he walked into the camp, brandishing his knife, and drove the inoffensive Celestials to an American store for protection. Had it not been for the interference of whites who accidentally met them on the trail leading to this place, two other parties of Chinamen would have been robbed and without a doubt murdered by Indians who had stopped and presented their weapons at them. Yesterday morning the little company consisting of four . . . their comrades having gone on ahead—started out and were followed by a villainous Indian with a gun and two knives. He was known to be one of the most desperate and heartless villains in the country and it was feared that he contemplated some outrage.

"Near noon one of the Chinese rushed back down the steep hill and over the bridge and stated as well as he was able that the Indian had stopped his party, making demands of provisions, etc., which they complied with until he wanted a pair of new boots which one of them had just purchased here. These were refused and he cut one of the party twice, severely, across the hand. The Johns then surrounded, disarmed and tied him to a tree and dispatched this messenger to ask what should be done with him. The Chinaman stated that they were ready to hang, shoot and cut him up or loose him, as the Boston men said. Meantime the news had spread among the Indians and almost before the Chinaman could recover his breath, Siwashes and Klootchmen were in arms, some with knives, others with guns, another with bow and arrow, and speeding silently away for a general fight.

"The scene presented was not without its interest; I had never seen a genuine war dance before, but here was a *bona fide* arrangement, somewhat extemporaneous, to be sure, and the steps anything but fanciful; for each hop was landing the dancer six or seven feet nearer the scene of the contemplated massacre. Two white men started out, accompanied by the chief of the tribe, and the Celestial messenger, and after half an hour, the sister of the prisoner came rushing, yelling back, assuming defiant and threatening attitudes, leaping high in the air, and brandishing her knife with a ferocity calculated to inspire another emotion than affectionate admiration in the breast of your correspondent.

"She was communicative only by signs for a long while, but before she spoke the news spread amongst the old women and children that her brother was tied and "memaloose" [dead]. It has been written that "Hell has no fury like a woman scorned", but the author of that passage had never seen a mad "Klootchman" [Indian woman] or he would have favoured the exception. Shortly after the completion of this act, the Siwashes gradually drew in, quietly putting their guns aside, and soon the white men with the chief and his prisoner approached.

"The chief here is a splendid fellow, and fair deer hunter, and I think—so long as there are plenty of whites in the country, at least— perfectly upright and desirous that justice should be done. He stated that this Indian was a scoundrel, and that he was disposed to let the white man deal with him; but the Boston men knew too well what the result would be to *them*, and the highway robber is now as free as I am and walks about as though he had accomplished a brave and mighty deed.

" . . . as soon as the Chief Constable, resident at Lillooet, learned the facts, which he did two or three days later, he repaired to the scene and administered a severe and just flagellation upon the offender, telling the Indians in their own language what it was for and assuring them that any future outrages upon Chinese would involve them in a war when they would all certainly be killed. He said the flogging was not strictly according to law, but if he had arrested the scoundrel and sent him below for punishment, the Indian would esteem it rather a reward than punishment, and the Government could not well afford to provision prisoners where regular 'muck-a-muck' [food] was sufficient inducement for a commission of repeated outrages."

As ghost towns go, these were not very satisfactory, and as we drove past the site of Bridge River it seemed as though we were chasing an Arthurian legend of old, and in particular those mysterious lost 140 parishes off the coast of Cornwall, which stretched from the mainland to the Scilly Isles, the shadowy land of Lyonesse.

> A land of old upheaven from the abyss
> By fire to sink into the abyss again.

Somewhere, we seemed to recall hearing a story of how at eventide if you listened closely from the shoreline, you could hear the bells of Lyonesse tolling the Angelus. It may not have been Lyonesse, it might have been some other land now reposing at the bottom of the sea, lost, and except for the musings of the poet and the story teller, forgotten.

29

Driving into the wonderfully rich valley of gold, a valley that holds such famous mines as the Bralorne and Pioneer in its bosom, we couldn't help comparing the fate of Minto City to these ancient, legendary cities.

But again, "why bother?" going to the trouble of going in, for there was obviously nothing to see, only a shimmering lake behind a power dam, a pall-like covering for a ghost town on which the dreams of countless investors once were pinned.

Minto City was born in 1934 and died in 1959 following a prolonged illness, but the foundations on which it rested went back to the year 1874 when John Cadwallader followed up earlier clues by some Italian miners working on Gunn Creek, and came upon a rich showing.

The town was founded by Warren A. Davidson, better known in the Bridge River country as "Big Bill". Until he died in 1958, Minto City was his, and like a father, he looked after it in good times and bad. But, unfortunately, there were more bad days than good.

At its peak nearly 800 persons lived in Minto, and it is said that more than a million in gold was taken out of the mine, but by 1942 it had petered out. The mine buildings were left to sag under the weight of the winters' snow and general neglect.

The miners left, although some said the only trouble with the Minto mine was that it hit a fault, and there's still plenty of gold in and around the property. War in the Pacific brought a new boom to Minto City, and the miners' homes were re-occupied, this time by re-located Japanese shifted from the coast as a security measure after the attack on Pearl Harbor.

With the end of the war the Japanese returned to the coast and houses in Minto became empty, nobody new moved in and activity in the area ceased.

Even before Big Bill plotted his townsite, the B.C. Electric Company had obtained flooding rights to the valley, and work had begun on construction of a tunnel through Mission Mountain to feed the generators at Shalalth on Seton Lake. But nobody thought that the valley where Minto City stood would be affected.

By September 8, 1960, when the Bridge River Power Scheme which had been slowed by depression and war, was completed, a shimmering body of water called Carpenter Lake backed by the Mission Mountain power dam had written *finis* to the valley, and Minto City lay drowned under 25 feet of water.

A remnant of the past, the McInnes House on the Cariboo Road, probably an outpost of old Fort Alexandria. During the gold rush it served as a "stopping place" on the road to the Cariboo diggings.

Fort Alexandria and Bullion

WE NOW HEADED BACK to the Fraser, following the tortuous course past The Fountain, and then headed over Pavilion Mountain and down to Clinton for a libation and collation at the old Clinton Hotel, the venerable landmark which, until the summer of 1958 when it was destroyed by fire, had served the wayfarer for nigh on a hundred years.

Under the spreading horns of a moosehead, two old timers were just about ready to come to blows.

"I tell you right here and now that Steve Tingley was the greatest man who ever set foot in the Cariboo!"

"Nonsense! J.B. Hobson's the man, and you just ask anybody, go ahead, ask anybody, and they will tell you the same. J. B. Hobson, that's who!"

The challenge was not, however, taken up, for the mere opinion of someone else would not change the devotion to Steve Tingley, the master stage coach driver and one-time owner of the famed B.C. Express Company, commonly called the BX. Nor would a denial by anybody that John Beauregard Hobson, of the great Bullion mine, was anything but the greatest have had any effect.

The fame of the Bullion and of J.B. himself is told up and down

31

the Cariboo Road and along the back roads. You hear it everywhere and the closer you get to the Bullion, the more you realize the extent of his great hydraulic operation and why, fifty years after his death, there are people still who will stand up and say he was the greatest.

Before following in the footsteps of Hobson, however, we had a call to make farther up the Cariboo Road to try and pin down a bit of Fort Alexandria's history, and to see if any "ghosts" remained of the old Fort, the last one to be erected by the North West Company prior to its merger in 1821 with the Hudson's Bay Company.

The first white man to reach this point was Alexander Mackenzie, who, on June 21, 1793, drew his canoes up in front of the Indian village and was told that beyond this point, and "every six or eight leagues" the Fraser was "encumbered with falls and rapids, some of which were very dangerous, and six of them impracticable." And so Mackenzie turned back towards Quesnel, and from there, headed for the "stinking lake" which he reached on July 22, thus becoming the first man to cross the continent "by land from Canada."

In 1821 a depot, or warehouse, was built at this site by the Northwesters, a granary was erected, and here, on the flat benchlands, the company's horses were wintered. In 1836 the post was removed to the other side of the Fraser, and in 1867 it was closed.

According to Gordon R. Elliot in his book *Quesnel; Commercial Centre of the Cariboo Gold Rush*, "between 1842 and 1846 the Hudson's Bay Company farm on Five-Mile Flat, east of the Fraser, operated a portable flour mill. Of U.S. manufacture, with stones two feet in diameter, it had been bought at Fort Vancouver, taken up the Columbia to Fort Okanogan by water, and from there by pack horse to this northern end of the brigade trail. The driving gear was built at Alexandria by a Canadian voyageur. In 1843 Alexandria was using 6500 bushels of grain a year for flour. Alexander Douglas McInnes obtained these Hudson's Bay Company farmlands in 1860."

With the discovery of gold on the Quesnel River, Fort Alexandria became better known than ever before. By October 1859 a log house was in course of construction and the miners were living in tents and brush houses and by September of the following year it was described as a "one horse town."

"The town lots of Alexander," said the *Colonist* on June 11, 1861 in a dispatch from nearby Beaver Lake, "are, it is said, to be sold shortly, although what good is to be derived from laying out a town where there are only a half dozen men puzzles people here rather."

And so, with this data in hand, we set out to find Fort Alexandria, a task much more complex than we had expected.

The Historic Sites and Monuments Board of Canada has erected a monument commemorating Alexander Mackenzie's voyage and the establishment of the Fort, but its location adds to the confusion, for it cannot, by its very position high above the river, be the site of the first Fort. (The second Fort was demolished in the late 1920s). But a couple of miles farther south, beside the Cariboo Road, stands a dilapidated building known as the McInnes House.

As we have seen, A. D. McInnes obtained the H.B.C. farmlands in 1860, and this building, it is said, was already in existence when the first miners came this way in 1859. So we can assume, although we cannot prove, that the McInnes House, later to be a stopping place along the road, is part of the old Fort Alexandria establishment. But still, where was the Fort?

Local tradition claims an old, sod-covered building down on the Indian reserve, and next to the church, one mile north and about half a mile west of the McInnes House, was part of the original fort. And so, if these traditions are correct, this building and the McInnes House are the ghosts of Fort Alexandria, and what stories they could tell! Stories of great pack trains—the brigades—taking precious furs from Fort St. James, to the north, down to Fort Vancouver on the lower Columbia, and of the momentous discovery of gold by Peter Dunlevy and Benjamin MacDonald on the Quesnel River. But let not your mind dwell on such things as talking walls, for ere long people will be talking of your mind.

The next puzzle in Fort Alexandria is the location of the "log house", the "one horse town" and "townsite."

Although Fort Alexandria, or Alexander townsite was surveyed in the 1860s by the Royal Engineers, there is no evidence it was ever placed on the market. Another local tradition says 21 lots were laid out, and a similar townsite of 20 lots was plotted at Soda Creek. But in some manner, the Fort Alexandria plans were substituted for those of Soda Creek, and for decades nobody knew the difference. This mistake was not noticed until the property at Soda Creek which should have been lot 21, was transferred, and then it was discovered there were differences in the size of the plans.

Obviously, this townsite would not be at the same point as the fur trading post, for the HBC did not give up their lands until 1860 when McInnes acquired them, and so the next best place would be to the north, beyond the historic cairn, probably close to where the present little Roman Catholic church stands.

Fort Alexandria had a "satellite," an establishment known as Fort Chilcotin. The thrill of "discovering" the ghost of this little-known Fort goes to Paul St. Pierre, now Associate Editor of the Vancouver *Sun*. He told about this adventure in history in the *Sun* for August 26, 1959:

"Found—the site of old Fort Chilcotin, forgotten and almost lost in a province which tends to forget its pioneers.

"It was the most exciting treasure hunt in my life. I started on the trail with an old, distorted map, drawn by some explorer of the last century.

"From this point, through the history books, by interviewing Indians and old settlers of the Chilcotin, it was a long chase.

"Nobody agreed.

"Fort Chilcotin had been an outpost of the bigger post at Fort Alexandria on the Fraser River, and the records show it was not a popular one. The Chilcotins were hostile to whites. They were bitter enemies of the Shuswap Indians on the other bank of the Fraser, killed them when possible and spurned the peace-making efforts of the Hudson's Bay traders.

"Among the scanty records that exist are letters from the half-breed clerk-in-charge, John McIntosh, pleading for more protection. (His fears caught up with him later in central B.C. He was murdered by the Sikanni.)

"The old map showed Fort Chilcotin at the base of Chilcotin Lake. But apparently there was never a post there.

"Some Chilcotin residents suggested the map called Puntzi Lake by the wrong name. But this, it turned out, was a private fur trading post of the mid-1800s. That trader was murdered, too. The Chilcotins were an unruly people.

"My best lead came from the book of missionary Father Morice, written in the last century. There were two references to the Fort, apparently contradictory. One referred to the post on Chilcotin River, and the other post was 'in the valley of the Chilco.'

"How could a fort be built on the banks of one river and in the valley of another?

34

"There could be only one answer—that it was near the junction of the two. And a mile upstream from where the powdery-green Chilco waters meet the clear stream of the Chilcotin I found the meadow they call Hudson's Bay Flat and rancher Gabriel Bayliff.

" 'We always assumed it was the site of Fort Chilcotin,' he said, 'But we never have known for certain, it could have been some little post of the Bay.'

"His father, Hugh Lane-Bayliff, rented the farm from the Bay after he had first pioneered in the Chilcotin in '87. Later the family bought it, District Lot 416 of Cariboo land recording district.

" 'It (the fort) was burned before my father came,' said Bayliff. 'We spot it in the meadows always by this particular grass that grows on the site. It's the same grass the Indian women used to weave baskets from.'

"There are two roughly square depressions in the ground, grown over with grass and prickly pear cactus. Nearby are numerous keekwillie holes where Indians once lived in their underground houses.

" 'Last fall,' said the rancher, 'Somebody found an old Hudson's Bay trade musket up on the hill there where the old trail leads to Alexandria. It was just leaning against a tree.'

"The ground in the flats is flecked with chips of obsidian and glassy basalt where the ancient arrowhead makers had worked.

"Nearby, where road crews had scraped gravel out for the nearby Chilcotin road, he showed me where two graves had been uncovered.

"A couple of whitened bones were still exposed and a piece of desiccated wood. The bodies had been buried in hewn-plank coffins.

" 'There was a pile of rock which we thought were the remains of an old chimney but they seem to have been scattered,' said Bayliff.

"He picked up a piece of blackened metal on the ground. I scraped it with a jackknife and the gleam of copper showed. It is probable that this is a piece of piah chickamin, red money, the copper pieces used in trade.

"Much of the story of this little outpost of the great fur trade empire remains a mystery. Probably all the pieces will never be fitted together.

"But the site at least now seems established.

"A telegram from Hudson's Bay House at Winnipeg says: 'Regret not much information here but according to our records Fort Chilcotin established about 1828 and abandoned 1872. Site purchased January

1941 by Gabriel Thomas Lane Bayliff, rancher of Alexis Creek, British Columbia.'

"It deserves a bronze plaque. Brave men lived there."

In picking up the trail of J. B. Hobson, we were also following the route taken by the miners of '59, and our object now was Dancing Bill's Gulch, the trickle of water which made J.B. famous, and to stand on the brink of a man-made canyon, two miles long and 200 to 300 feet deep. For all time this will be Hobson's memorial, and it will be shared with his subsequent successor at the Bullion, the late Ray F. Sharpe.

Dancing Bill's Gulch is located on the old road to Quesnelle Forks, the jumping off place for the discoverers of the wealth of Keithley, Antler, Harvey, Grouse and Williams creeks, and it was to reach these

J. B. Hobson of the Bullion Mine

Hydraulicking at the Bullion Mine during the Hobson era.

The Bullion pit: (on facing page) the eternal memorial to J. B. Hobson and his successor Ray Sharpe.

camps that we left the paved highway at the 150-Mile House, and bumped our way over the road which Hobson himself knew so well, past Crosina's store, the old 153-Mile, then the 158-Mile, or Mountain House (Parker's Place in Hobson's time), Big Lake, and into the beautiful valley in which nestles the Hamilton Place at Beaver Lake.

Perhaps Beaver Lake itself could be called a ghost town. In 1861 it was established as a stopping place, with two stores, the ever present gambling joint, and an animal market. The inn, or stopping place, was owned by a Frenchman, François Guy, and for many years, Beaver Lake was known far and wide as Guy's Place. In the course of time, all these buildings vanished, and the property came into the hands of the Hamilton family, descendants of an early Hudson's Bay trader.

As is the custom in this part of the country, the hand of hospitality

The ghosts of Bullion.

always is extended to the hungry and weary traveller if he comes to the door at meal time, and this particular wayfarer was ravenously hungry when he pulled up to the Hamilton Place. We sat down to dinner at the kitchen table with the ranch hands and what a feast! Platter after platter of different kinds of meats, bowls of steaming vegetables and mountains of home-made bread that just melted in your mouth—hardly a repast for a city-conditioned appetite. When it came time to ask for the bill, Miss Hamilton looked at us and said:

"Mister, you eat like a sparrow!" and then, almost apologetically, "would 50 cents be too much?"

For a moment we forgot about J. B. Hobson, "king of hydraulic mining" and the Bullion, our mind in awe and fear of the Cariboo sparrow!

A few miles distant we came to the first visible signs of our goal, Morehead dam, over which the road passes. Hardly recognizable as a dam, nonetheless it holds back the waters of man-made Morehead Lake, part of a system of waterways to supply a head for the Bullion's hydraulic pumps.

Six miles up the road, past Sam Prior's fretwork-trimmed, picturesque house at Hydraulic—a place which many people thought would boom back in 1911—we came to the unmarked crossroads. Taking the bush-lined road to the left, in a matter of minutes we were crossing the upper reaches of Dancing Bill's Gulch. A frightened deer, annoyed by our invasion of this his private domain, dashed across the weed-littered street, and with a kick of his hind legs, disappeared into the thick bush. The town was ours, and ours alone.

Dominating the lonely scene was the windowless, doorless, decaying ruins of Hobson's old home, a pathetic building which seems to cry out that it deserved a better fate. Down the gently sloping hill, towards the Pit, stand the remains of the bunkhouses, offices, dining hall and machine shops, the heart and soul of the mine, but now the soul has gone, the heart, long broken, and only the decaying body remains. But amongst the weeds, which never will be pulled, flowers bloom, filling the air with fragrance, proving that a small bit of the camp lives on defiantly, even though no one is there to admire the blossoms.

"The Bullion mine," said the *Report of the Minister of Mines* for 1942, "has come to the end of its life." The equipment was moved, and Dancing Bill's Gulch was returned to Nature.

A hundred years of history had passed that way before the afternoon we stopped to pay a visit.

Early in July, 1859 the Hudson's Bay Company fur brigade of 160 horses, bound for the coast from Fort St. James, reached Fort Hope on the lower Fraser bringing news of "considerable excitement 40 miles above Fort Alexandria." Billy Ballou's Pioneer Express messenger confirmed this, stating a good many miners were going up to the Canal, or Quesnel River, and coastal towns were feverish with excitement. Merchants in Port Douglas, for instance, closed up shop and headed north over the Cariboo Trail. At Lytton, in the canyon, a report to the Victoria *Colonist* in August noted the place was almost deserted. John Catherwood wrote to the *Colonist* that he was making $12 a day, but the water in the river was too high for serious mining operations, and then, J. J. May wrote to the paper: "I think there is a good show here to make a raise. Johnson (and other Canal River miners) says he is lying flat on his back with his heels cocked up towards the heavens, taking it easy waiting for the water to fall."

In the throes of this excitement was Dancing Bill, or to give him

The "Big House", built by J. B. Hobson, seems to cry out it deserved a better fate.

his full though seldom used name, Thomas Latham, a man who will make many colourful appearances in this odyssey in various parts of the province. In August of that eventful year, 1859, the Dancing Bill Company had a claim on the Horsefly River, as the South Fork of the Quesnel was known at that time, and according to the *Colonist* had "taken out as high as $110 a day with a rocker, and their last working yielded them an average of $75 per day and the entire claim pays them equally well. This is not an isolated case."

Dancing Bill moved on, seeking a better claim. Twenty years later a Chinese company was working the benchland at Dancing Bill's Gulch. A thousand feet back, and 125 feet above the Quesnel River, they discovered an old river channel running parallel to the main stream. These Chinese, it is said, took out at least $900,000 in values, until they too moved on, leaving a pile of tailings behind.

40

In 1892 a syndicate in Victoria listened with attentive ear to the elaborate plan of J. B. Hobson to "crush gravel from 2500 acres of old river bed." This scheme led to the formation of the Cariboo Hydraulic Mining Company, the following year, with Hobson as mine manager. In 1897 it was re-organized into the Consolidated Hydraulic Mining Company Limited, with a directorate made up largely of Canadian Pacific Railway officials.

The property covered about 10 square miles and it was thought that, potentially, at least, it would yield a tidy hundred million dollars in returns. The big problem was water to feed the hydraulic nozzles, and to solve it, Hobson began construction of a 21-mile canal, known as the South Fork Ditch, to tap Bootjack and Polley Lakes, drawing their waters to the great pumps installed at the mine. In the first six years of operation, $1,250,000 was recovered, but Hobson was after bigger returns.

In 1898 at a cost of $118,000, the Morehead dam and canal were constructed, and in the following year, the Morehead pooling reservoir was built at the head of Black Jack Gulch (named, incidentally, after Dancing Bill's partner). The more water Hobson got, the more he seemed to need, for even these great systems were unreliable, as they depended mostly on local rain and snow for their supply.

This shortage of water proved to be a continual source of trouble, and to remedy it, Hobson planned to tap Spanish Creek, ten miles distant, where he felt an abundance of water could be secured. But to do this, money would also have to be secured. For this, the directors turned to the great Guggenheim Exploration Company of New York, who, in 1906, took over control of the mine.

While Hobson was away back east attending to the negotiations for the deal, trouble was boiling in the camp. Blood had flowed, and a curse, a most terrible one, had been cast upon the mine, and if Hobson had been the slightest bit superstitious, the date July 9, 1906, could well have been blamed for the mountain of trouble which lay ahead.

Back in his California mining days, Hobson had a cook, Chung Kee You, or Sam Lock, as he was better known, and when the Bullion opened up, Sam Lock came north. Almost immediately he got into difficulties with the Highbinders of Quesnelle Forks, a particularly vicious tong, whose *forte* was blackmail. Under great pressure, Sam resisted all attempts by the tongsmen to force him to join, and was frequently threatened with dire consequences if he didn't. The tong had a man planted in the camp, a dining room servant by the name of Chew Hong, and frequently the two nearly came to blows.

At 4.30 p.m., as the men were turning to the camp from the Pit, they could hear screams coming from the boarding house. Rushing into the building, they found Sam Lock, a bread knife in hand, standing over the blood-covered figure of Chew Hong.

"May your evil spirit stay in your bones until they rot," Sam Lock was screaming at the body, repeating the curse over and over as the men pulled him away from the prostrate figure.

Sam Lock had been the friend of everybody in the camp, and there was nobody who wanted to see him turned over to the law. The elderly Chinese slipped away into the forest to hide, and at Cedar Point on Quesnel Lake, he built a semi-underground refuge. A reward of $300 was posted by the Provincial Police for his arrest, and although many men knew where he was hiding, and supplied the fugitive with food, their lips were sealed whenever the police were in the vicinity.

As for Chew Hong: the miners took the battered body and buried it in the tailings of the mine, and with him to his grave went the dreadful curse, "May your evil spirit stay in your bones until they rot."

Hobson was coming up the Cariboo Road from Ashcroft when he heard of the man-hunt for his faithful servant, and although many pressing problems awaited him at the camp, he dropped these to secure legal help for his friend of many years.

The offer of a $300 reward proved too tempting to a settler who lived near the mine; he told police where Sam Lock was hiding.

The accused came up for trial at Clinton the following October, but the case was set-over until May, and then to October, 1907, when he was found guilty.

On December 6, 1907 Sam Lock paid for his crime on the gallows at Kamloops, but in the meantime, the tide at the Bullion had turned, and some of the men thought back to the curse and the burial of Chew Hong and wondered.

All during 1906 Hobson's workmen had been engaged in tapping Spanish Creek, spending $200,000 of the Guggenheim's money, and as soon as the weather permitted, work at the Bullion was resumed.

However, just as Hobson's great dream was about to become a reality, a message was received from New York.

42

"The controlling interests of the company," said the *Report of the Minister of Mines* for 1912, "for reasons known to themselves only, ordered all work to be abandoned."

As might well be imagined, Hobson was thunderstruck. The abandonment of his cherished dream broke him in health and spirits. But in 1909 at the age of 65, he started to open up and equip some placer leases he held on his own on the North Fork of the Quesnel, near Spanish Creek. By the fall of 1911, all was ready for production, and as the 1912 *Report* said, he died on January 9, 1912, "just at the time when success seemed assured and without having been able to enjoy the fruits of years of arduous and efficient effort."

With the death of Hobson, the great house on the hill was uneasily occupied by a certain John Hopp, who, under the assumption that the Guggenheim interests had abandoned the property, drove in his own stakes. However, the New York interests apparently had sold the property to R. T. Ward, and a famous lawsuit resulted. The case was fought in the courts until 1919 when the Privy Council in London decided in favour of Ward. It was a hollow victory, for R. T. Ward. Although he was a clever mining man, he did not realize the great problem of the Bullion property, that is, that the mine was a huge, low grade deposit, and in consequence, a large volume of over-burden had to be removed economically.

In 1932 a Vancouver syndicate obtained control of the mine and brought in Ray F. Sharpe to operate it. Sharpe was not a mining man, but he knew water and how to make it work for him. For the next ten years, the old Hobson place was home and office to the Sharpes and the Bullion produced gold on a scale none of its previous owners had achieved. New lakes were tapped to bring water to the 11½ inch specially designed hydraulic monitors, and more than two million cubic yards of ground were removed each year. Costs were trimmed to under ten cents a yard, with recovery being about a quarter of a cent. It was, without a doubt, the most profitable, and most expensive low grade placer operation in the world. During 1938 the mine used more water per day than the entire city of Vancouver.

And finally, the Bullion simply ran out of gold and closed down. In time, the buildings will vanish, but the great Pit, an awe-inspiring wonder of man's genius for extracting the wealth of nature from the ground, will remain for ever and ever.

A view of Quesnelle Forks in its heyday.

Quesnelle Forks

GRASS GROWS in the streets, and the buildings of Quesnelle Forks are tumbling down from the weight of years. To the visitor, the old town presents a peaceful, tranquil appearance. But this is an outward, deceiving sign. Inwardly, the Forks is fighting for what little life remains, and it appears to be losing.

The river, which gave the town its very reason for being, is grimly exacting repayment for this favour, like a loan-shark grasping for all he can get. In this case, the Quesnel River is demanding all. Each spring, when the river rises during the annual run-off, it bites away at its banks, and a bit more of the town slips gently into the roaring, relentless river, and is gone.

Admittedly, this process is slow, but already it has claimed several buildings and washed out the bridge which once connected it with the main road from Beaver Lake, via Dancing Bill's gulch. Despite these encroachments of nature on the townsite, Quesnelle Forks must rank as being one of the most beautiful ghost towns in British Columbia, magnificently situated at the forks of the Quesnel River, surrounded by tree-covered mountains which seem to accentuate the loneliness of the town.

Quesnelle Forks was the first of the Cariboo gold camps, and began life in the "grand manner" of so many towns, taking unto itself the grandiose name Quesnelle City. It has also been known as Forks City, Forks of Quesnelle, Quesnel Forks, and just plain "the Forks."

Into Quesnelle Forks came the "big names" of the gold rush, William "Dutch Bill" Dietz, of Williams Creek, W. R. "Doc" Keithley, of Keithley Creek and Antler Creek fame, Billy Barker, the Cornish seaman who hit rich diggings at Barkerville, John Rose, and others whose names make up the colourful story of gold in the Cariboo. Here, until the Quesnel-Barkerville road was put through in 1865, came the greenhorns to mingle with the rough-cut miners. The good and the bad wandered along these streets that are now covered with grass. And some, nameless now, left their bones to moulder in the overgrown graveyard to the west of town.

Amongst the bad was Boone Helme, the notorious Montana bandit, who, it is said, killed three men between Keithley Creek and the Forks, and buried his loot under a cedar tree in what has since become known as Murderer's Gulch. Helme was later hanged by the Vigilantes in Virginia City along with other members of the infamous Henry Plummer gang, and he died without telling the secret of where the gold cache, said to be worth $200,000, lies.

And, somewhere in the mountains to the north, between the Forks and the Quesnel-Barkerville road, lies a lost mine. Two greenhorns found it, but as it paid only fifty cents to the pan, they hardly thought it worth bothering about. When they returned to the Forks, they found that 50 cents to the pan was a bonanza, but unfortunately, they couldn't find the spot again.

The story of Quesnelle Forks is almost a tale of two towns: the original settlement by white miners, founded in 1860 and destined, for a very short time, to be the largest "city" on the mainland; and the occupation by Chinese miners.

The Chinese — otherwise Celestials — followed the white miners wherever there was a discovery. And after the occidentals left, they stayed behind to clean up the claims. Low wages, hard work, loneliness and a lowly status were their lot, but it is their mark which we see in the Forks today.

A street scene in "modern" Quesnelle Forks. Building to the left was a store, in the distance a warehouse, and the third building was the Chinese Masonic temple or tong house.

The townsite was laid out by the Royal Engineers in 1861 as a supply centre for the myriad little creeks in the area which were turning out to be gold producers. On April 6, 1861 the Victoria *Colonist* said "Forks City contains about twenty stores and miners' cabins . . . and must in future years become the entrepot for all goods bound to Cariboo." Prices were high: a hundred pound sack of flour cost $68, a gold pan, $8, and a pick $6, or $7.50 with a handle. But nobody seemed to worry very much, as gold was plentiful, and one writer to the *Colonist* said "I have never met so many contented men in my life in any one place."

Amongst the first to arrive was a man, who, in 1895, signed himself "Cariboo" in a series of articles written for *The Province*, a weekly published in Victoria and now the Vancouver *Province*. He has left us an excellent description of life in the town, and in particular of a party. It was attended by Fred Black, a storekeeper at the Forks, Tom Barry and Sam Adler, destined to be the most famous saloon keepers in B.C., and "Abbott who ran what he was pleased to call a 'restaurant'.

"It was a small one room wooden shack. The furniture was all home-made and so constructed as to give one the idea that it was hurriedly fashioned on a Saturday night, or that the carpenter knew nothing of his business. In the centre of the restaurant was a six-legged table constructed of whip-sawn pine with forms to match. The culinary utensils were few and far between, but a roaring fire blazed on the hearth and made us feel happy."

It was Christmas, the first in this part of the Cariboo, and "Cariboo" went on to describe the festivities.

"We had all to lend a hand in the preparation of the feast, yet there was not so much to be done. Pork and beans was our chief dish, but not our only one; for we had some frozen beef, boiled, roasted, stewed and fried. The boiling pieces were knocked off with an axe, as were those intended for the stew pan, but the steaks were cut with a saw. So solid was the original junk frozen that we could scarcely tell whether we were working through bones or flesh until the frost thawed out. Then we had plum duff, without plums; plainduff, we called it. Next came slap (*sic*) jacks or pancakes, tea and coffee, whisky hot and whisky cold, brandy neat and two tins of sardines between ten of us. This was our first course. The second and third were without variation and like unto the first. It may be noted, however, that on this particular occasion, neither tea nor the coffee was in great demand.

"The chairman of the evening was friend Mike Brown, who, seated on an empty biscuit box, supported by a nail keg, filled the bill remarkably well . . . So successful was our dinner, that we formed a sort of mutual admiration society. The cook of the pork and beans was complimented by the fellow who looked after the slap jacks, who in turn, had a good word to say for the plain-duff man. Then Tom Barry put in a claim for his whisky hot, which was duly acknowledged by the boss of the stew job and all the rest of us . . . "

As new creeks were discovered, such as Keithley, Antler, Grouse and Williams, the miners moved on, and their place was taken by another wave of prospectors. For five years, the Forks prospered, but

47

then it went into decline, and for the rest of its life, the Forks was largely a Chinese settlement.

One of the main buildings standing today is the old Joss House, or Chinese Masonic Temple, a not very impressive building, but in its day, its interior was elaborately ornate. When we visited it the front door was locked with a giant padlock, but the back door was open wide so we went in. Around this building swirled all the activities of the Chinese population. It served as a court hourse to settle internal disputes, an employment bureau, community centre, funeral home and medical clinic, but now it is forlorn and rotting, with few signs of its intended role visible.

Set back from the main cluster of ancient log cabins is a great hollow-shell of a building, which the old timers in the area say was once a hotel and a place of tragedy.

The Chinese owner had a very beautiful wife, so the story goes, and was jealous of anyone who even looked at her. Often the little lady from the Flowery Kingdom threatened to run away, and so he built a fence around the back of the hotel, high enough to keep his wife from looking out and high enough to keep others from looking in. How long she endured this prison life is not recorded, but one day she removed a board and slipped away. It is to be hoped that she enjoyed her freedom for it was short-lived. A few days later, her beaten body was found beside a trail, and her husband was Number One suspect in her murder.

From time to time the white men came back to the Forks to make it their headquarters for the great hydraulic operations on the Quesnel River, but their return was far from being as flamboyant as it was in the beginning. Gradually, the fortunes of the Chinese began to fail, and it is said that by the early 1920s they were making about 20 cents a day per man in the once-rich gravels. In 1922, during the rush to nearby Cedar Creek at Likely, they left the old camp almost *en masse*. A few lingered on, and the last of the Celestials died in the winter of 1956, frozen to death on the trail from Likely to the Forks, a bottle of rum clutched in his hands.

A few old prospectors, still dreaming of making a great strike back in the hills, live with their memories in Quesnelle Forks. Perhaps, when they are gone, others will move into the log cabins beside the river bank, but the shadows have already closed in for the town and it seems unlikely that there is any future in store for it.

Chinatown, Keithley Creek, about 1902.

Kansas, Cedar City, Keithley Creek and Antler Creek

To THE PROSPECTOR this country was paradise. Every little creek was worth sampling, and some proved to be fantastically rich. Little towns sprang up overnight, and vanished, too, in fast time as new discoveries were reported. Each of these was but a stepping stone to the El Dorado that each and every miner felt in his bones existed. Perhaps, he thought he would be the one to find it; maybe tomorrow, or even the next day, and so he pushed on into the unexplored hills, seeking the elusive yellow metal. Many left their bones in crude graves beside a lonely trail—resting places no longer marked or even known to exist.

The old trails are overgrown and forgotten. It is possible today to travel in comfort to many of these locations, but imagination must be substituted for visible remains, as in most cases, there is little to show of the mining camps of long ago.

From Quesnelle Forks, the first spot to look for is Kansas, shown on old maps as being located at the south side of the Narrows where the Quesnel River leaves the lake. Apparently, Kansas lived and died without receiving any press notices, but according to Captain Norman Evans-Atkinson of Likely, who heard the tale from old-timers when he came into the country in the early 1920s, it was founded by the Dunlevy party and took its name from Kansas City, where Philadelphia-born Peter Curran Dunlevy at one time lived.

There were several buildings in Kansas, and on the ruins of one of these a three-storey lodge was built in the 1920s, but before it was opened the owner went bankrupt. The building was never used and local children used to play there imagining this was a castle of old. As time went on the building decayed and as a safety measure, it was burned down in 1962. A nearby cabin may be part of Kansas, but alas, only it knows the truth.

A few miles down the lake, at the mouth of Cedar Creek, once stood Cedar City, the site of which is on Captain Evans-Atkinson's property. Its birth was announced in the *Cariboo Sentinel*, Barkerville's little newspaper, on July 8, 1867.

"CEDAR CREEK—A new town has sprung up a few hundred feet back from the lake; it contains two stores, one kept by Mr. Isaac Lipsett, and the other by Mr. Gibson; one restaurant and a butcher's shop, kept by a son of the Flowery Kingdom. The boys speak very highly of him, as he gives unlimited "jaw-bone" to anyone who applies for it, which is saying a great deal for a Mongolian. Mr Sellars [Jim Sellars, formerly of Beaver Lake, a partner of Peter Dunlevy] is putting up the most substantial building in the camp and will be ready to open it as a hotel in a week or two."

In the great fire of 1869 which swept through the area, leaving only a stand of cedars at Cedar Point in its wake, Cedar City was destroyed, but it was not forgotten.

During the "hungry thirties" when hundreds of men tried to earn a living by prospecting along the banks of the Quesnel River, the site of Gibson's store was pointed out, and eagerly the miners dug into the ruins and panned the dirt in the hopes that some gold might have dropped through the floor cracks.

It is not known whether much gold was recovered in this way, but in all likelihood it was pretty lean pickings. However, at Cedar Point, two gold caches were discovered in a stump.

Nineteen miles from the site of Cedar City a little stream flows into Cariboo Lake called Keithley Creek, named after one of the "greats" in the early annals of the Cariboo. He was W. J. "Doc" Keithley.

Keithley Creek is known not only as a stepping stone on the long road to the eventual bonanza on Williams Creek, but as headquarters for Veith & Borland, once owners of the 150-Mile House, and, in the early days of B.C., one of the largest mercantile houses in the country. Today it is a sorry picture of its former self. The hotel and beer parlour, symbols of a later day, have closed and the building is boarded up. And when that happens in the Cariboo it is a pretty sure sign that dry rot has gone far in the town! A few headboards peak from behind tall grass in the cemetery, and perhaps a cabin or two in the bush can be dated to Keithley Creek's golden era, but that is all.

The tide of miners reached Cariboo Lake late in the fall of 1859, and, for the dual reasons of good prospects and a fast approaching winter, a cluster of rough buildings or cabins was thrown up to form the nucleus of a town. The saloon keepers and the gentlemen of the gambling fraternity arrived shortly afterwards and Keithley became noted for its frontier recreational palaces. The *Colonist*, reporting on October 26, 1860 on the goldfields, said of the Creek that "the gambling halls were going full blast."

During 1860 and 1861 Keithley was in its prime, although, according to the Victoria newspaper on July 21, 1861 it consisted only of five log houses and about 20 tents. In the surrounding hills there was great activity. The town's namesake, Doc Keithley, along with John Rose, Sandy MacDonald and George Weaver, had found, in the fall of 1860 a gold laden stream about 18 miles away. They tried to keep their discovery a secret, but according to Agnes Laut in her book *The Cariboo Trail*, when two of them went back to Keithley for supplies, either they said something by mistake, or their silence gave them away, anyway, the cat was out of the bag, and in short order, Keithley Creek and even Quesnelle Forks were deserted. All eyes were now on Antler Creek, and when, in the following spring, the Gold Commissioner arrived to register the claims, he found the Keithley party living in a cabin, while the rest of the camp held down their claims by living in holes which they had dug into the ground.

Thus was born Antler City, named because the discoverers found a set of deer antlers here. And Keithley Creek, no longer the head of the golden trail, fell back and took its place merely as a stepping stone and as an oasis in the bush.

When the news reached the coast of the Antler strike, there was a furor of excitement, and in June 1861, when the season opened, the *Colonist* noted that buildings in New Westminster were covered with placards reading "selling off to go to Cariboo."

By August of that eventful year of 1861 Antler was getting to be quite a "city." The correspondent for the *Colonist* said "new houses are being put up every day . . . and I don't know how many drinking saloons are being constructed." Gambling was openly carried on, with four monte tables in operation and "one dealer realized a very respectable stake in a short period." Respectable may not have been the most appropriate adjective to apply.

Life in Antler was described by "Argus" in a letter to the newspaper on August 19:

"A band of minstrels perform here two or three times a week and together with the exciting recreations of bucking at *monte moule* and draw poker, tend to enliven us not a little. Money has lost its value in the mines, and a twenty-dollar gold piece is looked upon much in the same way that a two-and-a-half would be in Victoria. It is an exhilarating sight to see natty pyramids of American double eagles changing hands in the saloons and impresses us with the idea that the country is safe and gold mining not yet played out."

However, from the beginning, Antler was in trouble. While the gambling games were going on, the Gold Commissioner, Philip Henry Nind, was warning that the town was built on miners' ground and that all the houses must be moved to Sawmill Flat, three miles away. In September, a miner named Patterson, began sluicing in the town and, said the *Colonist*, "altercations are constantly ensuing between the proprietors of houses and Patterson." At the same time, Antler was faced with this disturbing problem, it was announced that "the name of the town of Antler has been changed to Munroville, after its first settler."

"It bids fair," said the *Colonist* on September 19, 1861, "to become the largest mining town in the sister Colony, and contains ten saloons, seven general stores, two blacksmith shops, a sawmill, a shoemaker and a butcher shop."

Although the gamblers were quick at taking the gold from the miners, they were, like a modern phrase, "all heart."

"The sporting fraternity," said the *Colonist* on October 28, 1861, "have very generously come forward and bought a house which is to be turned into a hospital. There are at present three men staying there on the sick list. The same parties also got up a subscription amounting to $1200 as a provision for the necessary wants of the sufferers."

Prices in Antler that year were fantastic. A box of matches cost $5.00; rubber boots, a very necessary item in the shafts, were $50 a pair, and 100 pounds of flour cost $112.

Despite these charges, Dennis Cain wrote this notable "Dear John" letter, which appeared in the *Colonist* for August 26:

"Dear John:

. . . you are no doubt doing well—$100 per month and steady work is not bad; but you can do better up here. No less than ten of our Horsefly boys are doing well—have struck it rich. You know I was dead broke last Fall; now I have a claim paying from $75 to $100 per day to the hand, a store on this creek, and a pack train carrying goods from Quesnelle City here. Take my advice and leave for the up-country at once, and if you don't strike a claim to suit you, I will pay you $125 per month and board to work for me—so you have a good thing anyway! . . ."

Like the others, Antler soon faded, and on July 23, 1865, following several other "big strikes" in the area, the *Colonist* referred to Antler as a "ruined city" with only one company at work. It had a brief comeback, but it was never the same.

The temperance men might say the doom of Antler was in its saloons. Perhaps. But the fate of Antler, like the Forks, Keithley and Cedar City lay deep against the bed rock of a couple of creeks less than a dozen miles away. The saloons' role in the decline of Antler was that they contributed to unlocking secrets a little earlier than they normally might have leaked out. Take the case of Richard Willoughby, as recorded in the *Colonist* for July 30, 1861:

"Mr. Willoughby," said the newspaper, "partook too freely at Antler and let the cat out of the bag while in a temple of Bacchus, and 200 followed him over the hills to his new strike, and an equal number came soon afterwards.

"Mr. Willoughby took to a stump and putting his two hands on his sides began, Demosthenes-like, to deliver himself of a burden of oratory—Gentlemen, said he, here I am! Look at me! I am only a common man, like you fellows, but (a growl from the audience and the speaker took a long breath) yesterday I was like you fellows, a poor common man but (another growl from the common audience) today I am rich! I have struck the Great Lowhee Creek and there is ground for all of you fellows. (The orator was prevented from proceeding by cries of "Pull him down, shoot him, hang him, boys!") And so terminated Richard Willoughby's first attempt at public oratory."

The Lowhee became one of the great placer operations of the Cariboo, and in an indirect way, provided one of the main clues to the opening and developing of the Cariboo Gold Quartz property at Wells during the early 1930s.

Willoughby had been a '58er to Yale where a secret society was formed amongst the miners called the Grand Lowhee Association. A member being initiated in the mysteries of the order was induced to confess to the committal of a robbery at Emory Bar. The creek above the Lowhee was named Brock, after the pass-word of the Association.

A few months earlier, another '58er, William "Dutch Bill" Dietz, talked too much in Antler, and another step forward to El Dorado was taken.

Richfield

THERE WAS a rumour afloat that the road from Keithley to Barkersville, "over the hump" was closed for lack of a bridge, and so we turned back and headed for Quesnel and the historic road into Barkerville.

Parking our vehicle in front of the new Barkerville Museum we hastened through the restored ghost town to the Theatre Royal to catch the next stage coach to Richfield (true). Enroute the driver stopped at Art Pederson's dude gold mine, where we decided to recoup some of our expenses by indulging in a bit of prospecting. For fifty cents we got a pan filled with dirt and were escorted to a sluice box and went to work. For our half-dollar we got back about 40 cents in gold, which

Government Building at Richfield during early days of the Williams Creek mining boom.

was pretty good, but when the initial excitement of our "big strike" wore off, we soberly realized that this ratio of expense and profit would never defray any costs. But Art Pederson was making money.

This section of ground was part of the historic Morning Star claim, one of the great claims along Williams Creek, and hundreds of people each day were experiencing the never to be forgotten thrill of extracting gold from the earth's storehouse.

Meanwhile, back at the stage coach, the driver was growing impatient with his *nouveau riche* passengers. A mighty man, he, for he was able to persuade his fares to leave the gold in the ground and get on with the trip.

All around us were the scars of hydraulic mining, and the neat piles of tailings left by the early miners. And the little stream we were following was often called the "richest creek in the world." Here "Dutch Bill" Dietz made his famous strike, and here, in Richfield which grew as a result of Dietz' discovery, the famed Cariboo judge, Matthew Baillie Begbie, delivered a firm but fair justice to the malefactors.

Begbie's Court House, built in the 1860s, is the sole surviving building of old Richfield, and like Barkerville's buildings, it is being preserved by the provincial government.

It was in early February 1861 that Dutch Bill and his party set out from Antler Creek, through the deep snow and over the hump into the valley of a nameless little stream.

"They found prospects on the north-west side of the creek," said the Victoria *Chronicle* for November 5, 1863, "varying from ten to thirty cents to the pan near the bedrock. After that one of the party sunk a hole on the east side . . . and obtained a similar result. Night coming on, and much time having been lost through having but one pick (the other having been left at Antler because they thought that shovels would be more required for stripping off the snow), they abandoned their work for that day and lit a fire to cook supper. But Dutch William, restless and enterprising, left the others basking before the burning logs, and travelled up the creek until he found the bare bedrock cropping up in the stream. He tried one panful of gravel, but obtained none of the precious metal. He tried another taken from the side near where there was a high ledge, and to his great delight found himself rewarded with a dollar to the pan. The gravel was frozen hard to the rock and when detached with difficulty thawed in the cold stream. Time passed quickly and he was soon obliged by darkness to return to his campfire. He showed his companions the prize he had obtained, but they, possibly hardly believed his statement, for they determined to return to the Forks."

One of those who accompanied Dutch Bill was the man who signed the name "Cariboo" to a series of weekly articles in the *Province* in 1895. His story of that momentous day differs slightly in some details from the *Chronicle* story, but it tells how the creek got its name.

"When we had our general meeting at the camp-fire according to arrangement we again compared notes and submitted our samples. The showing by Dutch Bill was the richest of the lot, about $1.50 to the pan, and on the motion of Mike Brown, it was decided to call the place Williams Creek. Someone was about to propose another name, but Bill pleaded "If you vil call it by me, I vill hoppen for you de very first case of vine vot comes into de country." There was no opposition after this. "Prosperity to Williams Creek" was drunk in tea out of tin goblets. "Little did we think we were naming the richest creek that the Golden Cariboo boasts of."

Dutch Bill returned to Antler for a pick and further supplies, and soon after his arrival, the miners guessed he had a secret and they decided to trail him.

The historic Court House at Richfield, where Judge Matthew Baillie Begbie dispensed his stern justice to the malefactors of the Cariboo.

"Leaving his companions to bring up stores," continued the *Chronicle*, "he started back at daybreak for his new creek — making the distance in the wonderfully short time of three hours over an unblazed trail. But his strenuous exertions were unavailing; the whole population of Antler had tracked his steps, and within two or three hours after his arrival, the whole creek was staked off into claims over ground covered with eight feet of snow.

Poor Dutch Bill, his was the poorest claim on the creek, and when he died in 1877 it was a pauper's death.

From Dutch Bill's discovery, the merchants, *et al* of Antler moved and set up shop in the new town of Williams Creek, which in 1862 was to be changed to Richfield.

RICHFIELD: "The name of the town of Williams Creek," said the *Colonist* on October 14, 1862, "has been changed to that of Richfield by Lieut. Palmer, Deputy Commissioner of Lands & Works. The Grand Jury at Williams Creek recommended that the place should be called Elwyntown, after the Gold Commissioner of the District, but Lieut. Palmer seems to have thought Richfield more euphonious and appropriate."

A description of any mushrooming mining camp would cover Williams Creek, or Richfield, in its early months. There were the usual saloons, restaurants, stores and blacksmiths. By July 1863, it was well on its way to becoming a place of importance, and Isaac Dixson could boast in the Victoria newspapers that his "large and commodious Richfield Restaurant" was the "only house in Cariboo where cleanliness and quiet combined with politeness and attention to their personal comforts can really be secured by the miner."

"The style of architecture here," the *Colonist* said on July 10, 1863, "is peculiar in its order. It is neither Doric, Ionic nor Corinthian, but decidedly Columbian. It is quite as primitive as any of the above orders, but not so classic. The relative properties of capital, column and base never trouble the mind of the Richfield builder. The Government have put up a new building for the Commissioner. It far surpasses in magnitude any of the other log and mud structures which humbly show their roofs and smoke their chimneys around it. It has glass windows—by the way, a dash at a pane of glass here is an expensive luxury, every crash which tinkles the tympanum is music at the rate of $3 per 8 x 10 pane. People in glass houses (here above all other places) should not throw stones."

"I may mention," the newspaper account continued, "that two grand balls have been given. The few ladies on the creek (by the way there are about ten who have come up no doubt for reasons best explained in the book of "Common Prayer") graced the festive scene with their lovely presence. The viands were of the choicest, every individual getting his "regular beans, you bet!" I insist that the wines were not made of burnt sugar and lightning, Anglice alcohol. Another entertainment is soon to be given. No cards, as paper is scarce, and the entertainers can't write and many of the invited can't read. Good reasons these."

We get another description of Richfield from the August 3 *Colonist*:

"There is nothing very prepossessing in its appearance to a person about to enter it, probably not as much as some of the mining towns of Australia or California; and its general importance among the Cariboo miners chiefly arises from it being the point of ingress and egress to, and from the mines.

"When I first arrived at Richfield there was nothing to be seen at that time. The houses were dilapidated and uninhabited, except for one or two stores and saloons that had been doing a good business all winter. The only one of any importance belonged to Beedy & Co. whose business controlled all the others. It is singular to see in the space of a few months what progress has been made in its appearance.

"Several stores, hotels, etc., have been built and opened and nothing wanting that could possibly be procured to appease the appetite of the hard-working miner; but if his pocket cannot come up to relieve the cravings of his appetite, he must be content to live on Cariboo turkey (bacon) and Cariboo strawberries (beans) and a happy man is he whose pockets can command this nutritious though simple fare. As for myself, I have left my partiality for delicacies in Victoria, to be unpacked and called in requisition when I again reach the vicinity of the St. Nicholas or the French Hotel.

"Richfield can at present boast of one street—and such a street! Its houses may be classed as verbs; i.e., they are neither active or passive, but certainly regular, irregular and sometimes defective. The sidewalks are of different grades, and in some parts, where a sidewalk would be most needed none exists. The hills on each side of the creek, which is very shallow at present, are covered in many parts with the tents, shanties, etc. of the mining population, and I assure you, they have a very pleasing appearance, being built in such different styles of rustic architecture."

Thus was Richfield, and in one of the saloons in the year 1862, amid the clamour of the throng, might be heard the voice of a "Cariboo immortal," Billy Barker, singing

> I'm English Bill,
> Never worked, an' never will.
> Get away girls,
> Or I'll tousle your curls.

The El Dorado was at hand.

A cattle drive down Barkerville's single muddy street.

Barkerville and Camerontown

BARKERVILLE was in a festive mood on August 13, 1962. It had a centennial to celebrate, and even the Premier of the province, the Honourable W. A. C. Bennett, was in town for a special meeting of the cabinet. A hundred years earlier, Billy Barker struck it rich, and as Bishop Hills noted in his journal, "all went on a spree for several days, excepting one Englishman, well brought up."

It had been many a long day since the old "gold capital of B.C." had seen such a throng walking along its dusty main street. What must the ghosts of Barkerville have thought? To find the answer we followed our usual custom on visiting Barkerville to stop in for tea with Fred Tregillus, the last of the Cornish miners, and his family. He had come to Barker-ville in 1885, and had known Billy Barker, Cariboo Cameron, Ned Stout, one of Dutch Bill's partners, Wellington Delaney Moses, and many other "originals" on the Creek. Miss Lottie Bowron, daughter of John Bowron, an argonaut of '62 and later Gold Commissioner, was also there, and the talk around the little circle was of the old days. Yes, they thought the ghosts of yesterday would be pleased with the restoration of Barkerville, and with that understanding we set out to see the "new" town and to compare it with the "old" pre-restoration Barkerville we had come to know and love.

A month after our little tea party, the bell in the steeple of St. Saviour's Church—the miners' church—tolled for Mr. Tregillus, and he was placed with the other argonauts in the little Barkerville Cemetery. He was just one month short of reaching the century mark himself.

In effigy, Billy Barker still exults over his tremendous find, at the precise spot where, back in 1862, he reached the 52-foot level of his shaft and struck pay dirt. Poor Billy! With his newly found wealth he went down to Victoria and there married a widow by the name of Elizabeth Collyer. She took him for whatever she could get, and so did the saloon keepers. Within a short time Barker was broke, his wife skedaddled, and he was no longer warmly received in the saloons. He died in 1894 in Victoria, a pauper, his last days being made easier by the generosity of J. B. Hobson of the Bullion.

A few months after Barker made his strike, John A. "Cariboo" Cameron

*St. Saviour's
Anglican church.*

61

struck it rich a mile below the Barker shaft. Tragedy of a different kind from Barker's stalked that operation. The claim was owned by Cameron and his gentle wife Sophia, but before the richness of the ground could be proved, the rigours of the rugged life she had chosen to follow, claimed her and she succumbed from "mountain fever." The richness of the claim was astounding, but it brought no happiness to the man who found it. His beloved Sophia was gone. In March 1863 he disinterred her body, and made plans to send it home to Cornwall, Ontario. It was a hard trip down to Victoria, and in that city the body rested for nine months before being sent once again on its way. On its arrival in Cornwall just before Christmas it was rumoured Sophia was not in her coffin, instead it was filled with gold. Again the body was disinterred, and when the ghoulish story was disproved, Sophia Cameron was finally allowed to rest in peace. But not her husband. He made one bad investment after another, and soon was as broke as the day he went into Cariboo. Years later, in a vain hope of recouping his losses, Cariboo Cameron returned to Barkerville where he died penniless on November 7, 1888. He is buried in the little graveyard that stands in a grove of trees above his famous claim.

Around these two men and their claims grew the twin towns of Barkerville and Camerontown. Both were lusty and wide-open, but it was simply a question of the survival of the fittest. After a short life-span, Camerontown vanished, and now only a sign marks its location. Barkerville went on, to be known up and down the coast as the largest "city" north of San Francisco and west of Chicago. But it, too, was to become a ghost town.

In Barkerville's heyday, fortunes were made almost overnight. The Steele claim yielded 409 ounces per day, or $6,544; Cunningham's produced nearly $2,000 a day, and the Adams yielded each of its three partners a total of $40,000. The Diller on one occasion yielded 200 pounds of gold, worth $38,000, in one day, and the Caledonian was known to have produced $5000 to $6000 in gold within a 24-hour period. From a 120-foot claim, a total of $100,000 was taken out by the Neversweat Company, and the Ericsson had a weekly yield averaging 1400 ounces.

No wonder Williams Creek became known as the "richest stream in the world," and no wonder thousands flocked to this golden town in search of their fortunes. But the figures were deceiving, even though they caught the imagination of the world, for they were the rare exceptions

Billy Barker, pictured at Quesnelle Forks shortly before he died.

The Barker Claim as restored in the Barkerville park.

rather than the rule. James Anderson, the "poet laureate of the Cariboo", summed up the lot of the majority in one of his *Sawney's Letters*:

> *You'd maybe like to ken what pay*
> *Miners get here for ilka day*
> *Jist twa pound sterling, sure as death—*
> *It should be four—atween us baith*
> *For gin ye count the cost o' livin'*
> *There's naething left to gang and come on;*
> *And should you bide the winter here,*
> *The shoppy-buddies'll grab your gear.*
> *And little wark ane find to do*
> *A' the lang dreary winter thro'.*

Those who took the "big money" out left nothing behind, so Barkerville is the town of the poor but honest miner, and the tradesman, like Sandy MacArthur the blacksmith, Johnny Knott, the carpenter, Dr. Hugh Watt, MD, the town's doctor, and Wellington D. Moses, the nosey little barber who jotted down in his diary everything he saw, and some of the things were none of his business. Barkerville is also the town of the Chinese, who lived a life far different from the Occidental miner.

It was difficult to imagine that just three years previously, Barkerville was a ghost town, just like Quesnelle Forks. Now actors, and people from Wells, brought reality to the once-deserted street. Ladies promenaded in fancy costumes and men wore bushy whiskers which would come off the minute the centennial celebrations were over—or so their wives said.

There was something for everybody to enjoy in the town, whether it was a ride on the stage coach, or a plate of Cariboo turkey and Cariboo strawberries in the Wake-Up Jake Coffee Saloon. The two other saloons were open, but they were just show places, for alas, Barkerville is dry, and this could well be a point which the ghosts would criticize.

Building after building in the old town is coming alive; the Bowron House, an example of Barkerville's gracious living, the Gold Commissioner's office, Moses' barbershop, Dr. Watt's office, MacArthur's blacksmith shop, and the Kelly and Nicol Hotels, and in Chinatown, the opium dens, gambling houses, cabins, stores and Masonic temple.

And over all these, looks the steeple of St. Saviours, built a year after the first Barkerville was destroyed by fire in 1868.

If you let your mind wander in Barkerville, you can imagine you are witnessing things which happened long ago. It's not difficult, for the people

Camerontown was named for 'Cariboo' Cameron.

responsible for the face-lifting have done their job well, and the magic spell they have cast over the old buildings does strange things to your senses.

Why, you can even blush in your imagination as your mind's eye sees a burly miner pick a hurdy gurdie girl up, toss her on his shoulders and shout with joy as she dances with her feet on the ceiling. Or you'll suffer excruciating pain as you watch a poor miner getting his teeth fixed in a dentist's chair. And the lovely lady playing the piano in the Bowron House is not merely a manniken, but a charming accomplished pianist playing a delightful Mozart melody.

Barkerville is more than just a collection of shacks, it is a memorial to all who have toiled for gold, not only in the Cariboo, but throughout the province, and it is a fitting one.

The Heron Claim on Grouse Creek, 1867.

Grouse Creek

LEAVING THE GAY Barkerville festivities behind, we drove past the great Cornish water wheel next to the Museum, crossed Williams Creek, and headed up Conklin Gulch to the forgotten ghost town of the Cariboo, Grouse Creek, or Grousetown, a distance of only about three miles.

Tales of the Grouse Creek War and the Lost Heron Lead were ringing in our ears as Fred Ludditt of Wells, who knows the creek intimately, drove us up the road which leads to the deserted Cariboo Hudson mine, and if the bridges are in order, to Keithley Creek. As we bumped along the seldom used road he pointed out the sites of old mining shafts, and the remains of the first steam engine used in Cariboo mining, dating from about 1897, at the unlucky Houser shaft on Canadian Creek. Here, a side road branches to the right, and in a few minutes we were on Cornish Bench, a rich bit of ground which in the 1860s was giving nine ounces of gold per day to the man for eleven Cornish miners. Immediately below was Grouse Creek and a huddle of decaying buildings.

At the same time as Dutch Bill's famed Williams Creek was being called a "humbug", miners were getting good returns from Grouse, but it was not until 1865 that the stream proved its worth. The secret of the creek was not in the present creek bed, but in an ancient channel, and it was in the "hill diggings" that a Mr. Sneddon struck it rich on the Discovery claim late in 1865.

A writer for the *Colonist* on May 4, 1866 said he saw Robert Hutchinson, foreman of the Discovery, "take out of the dirt with his candle stick a half a dozen pieces of gold from 25 cents to a dollar and a half. This was out of not more than a handful of dirt."

By 1865 the Cariboo was ready for a new strike. Barkerville had lost its lustre to the adventurous, and the only hope in the camp was the possibility of buying into a claim, or working for wages. The Kellys of Barkerville established a restaurant on the Creek and the *Colonist* said, on November 2, 1865, that business appeared to be brisk along the creek "if we may judge from the fact that a storekeeper sold out a cask of liquor in two or three days".

The original Grousetown which came into being in '61 was a mile or so downstream, but no landmark remains to mark its site; it is the town of '65 which survives. According to Mr. Ludditt, the two remaining cabins in good shape date back to the early days of this camp. The largest of these, built by a man named Jarvis, whose fabulously rich Mary claim was only a stone's throw away, was lived in until 1955 by a man named Paul Gaines, or Gagnon, who in 40 years in the Cariboo had sunk 42 shafts, the deepest being 70 feet. He was an active 75 years of age when he died.

A legend has grown up around the old Gaines place, and in the days before pay day when the family coffers are getting low, we often wonder whether we walked over old Gaines' cache of gold without realizing it. Mr. Ludditt says he used to go over from Wells to drive Mr. Gaines into town, and the old man would excuse himself for ten minutes or so, go into the bush, and always came back with a good-sized poke of gold in his pocket. He told Mr. Ludditt that before he died he would give him the secret of the location of the cache, but this wasn't to be. Death sealed his lips, and the cache, if it wasn't "played out", awaits a lucky finder.

Between the Gaines cabin and the other, adjoining it, are the ruins of Anthony McClanneden's dance hall, a building which probably was only about 28 x 30. This need occasion no surprise, as it had a good sized "wine cellar". Farther downstream, a ruined barn-like building is open to the elements, and in what was once the Chinese section of town, are the remains of Wing Louie's store, just a pile of timbers erratically covering a depression in the bottle-strewn ground.

Across the street from McClanneden's place are the scars of the Heron claim, the richest and still the most controversial bit of mining ground on the creek.

In 1867 the Heron company received a franchise to build a flume extending for several hundred feet along the creek to pick up water and carry it past their ground to keep the workings at least reasonably dry. This enabled the Heron people to take out between 50 and 100 ounces of gold per day, and it also sparked the rush that put Grouse on the map after four years of more-or-less idleness.

A company, known as the Canadian, staked some ground which the Heron group claimed was covered by their franchise, and began to work it. The Heron company took steps to see that the trespassers were removed, and in this they were backed by the Gold Commissioner. The Canadian's operators found they had outsmarted themselves.

Early in the trouble they obtained from Judge Begbie an order setting aside any future appeal from the Gold Commissioner's Court, and now that the Gold Commissioner was on the side of the Heron company they found their appeal was tossed out because of the earlier decision.

Nevertheless they refused to withdraw, and when an order was issued for their arrest, the Canadians resisted with force.

H. M. Ball, the Gold Commissioner, then swore in a couple of dozen special constables to enforce his order, and the Canadians reciprocated by gathering together a force of about 400 men. Uneasiness reigned along the creek, and the heavily out-numbered forces of law and order were helpless. They called upon Governor Frederick Seymour for assistance.

The climax of the crisis came on July 19, 1867 when the forces of the Canadian company charged at the Heron men and drove them not only from the disputed property, but also from the undisputed Heron workings. The victors thereupon set to work and took out gold variously reported as totalling from 100 to a thousand ounces per day, working on a round-the-clock basis. It was the intention of the Canadian company to work the ground out before the dispute was settled, and to do this they formed a subsidiary company called the Sparrowhawk which took over the whole Heron ground.

The ghosts of Grouse Creek lie forgotten in the bush.

Seymour acted quickly, and on August 7 he paid a personal visit to Richfield, the first time a head of government had ever come to Cariboo. There he met representatives of the two sides and tried to induce the Canadian company to deliver the 12 feet of disputed ground to the government, and to pay over to some public official the amount of gold taken out, and at the same time, surrender to the authorities those men who had balked the original court order.

Eight men gave themselves up and were sentenced to three months in jail, but the remaining members of the company took up a petition and the sentence was reduced to two days. When Governor Seymour left, his stature in the eyes of the miners had greatly diminished; he had failed to give justice where justice was needed, and, by his decision, had encouraged rowdyism.

On hearing rumblings of discontent, Seymour issued a special commission to Chief Justice Joseph Needham to go to Richfield and bring the dispute to a close. On September 15, 1867 the trial began, and the next ten days were lively ones. Finally, Needham ruled in favor of the Heron company, ordering the ground, as well as the gold held by the court, to be returned.

The troubles of the Heron company, however, were by no means over. Suddenly, and dramatically, the rich ground "gave out" and not even a trace of gold could be found.

Fortunes have been spent searching for the Lost Heron lead. It may be a mile away, it might be on top of a mountain, or it might be one shovelful away, who knows? But nearly every summer, somebody will come into Wells or Barkerville, and take the road up Conklin Gulch to look for it. The ways of a prospector never change—the gold is there, and why couldn't he be the one to find it?

PART II

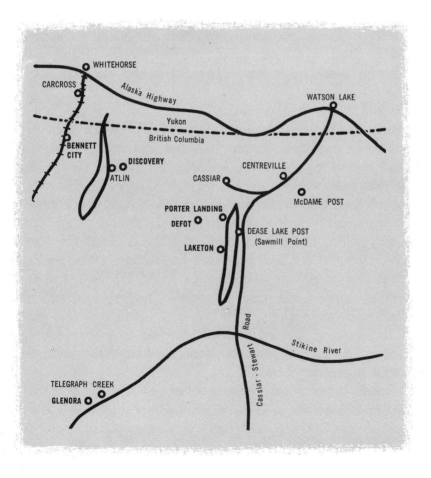

Dease Lake Post

COMFORTABLY SEATED in Canadian Pacific Airlines' turbo-jet *Empress of Lima* we could see the tips of the glacially scarred Stikine Mountains, thousands of feet below us as the great white plane skimmed across the southern Yukon Territory from Watson Lake to Whitehorse. And beyond the Stikine Mountains lay the spreading Cassiar plateau in which nestles Dease Lake, and beyond, cutting it deeply, the mighty Stikine River flows swiftly and tortuously to the sea. A lonely land this, rich in natural resources and scenic beauties. A hundred years ago it was better known than it is today. But with the building of the Cassiar-Stewart Highway it is making a comeback.

In its opening chapters it was a land of fear, and there is a familiar ring today to the fear which Robert Campbell felt as he entered the Cassiar in 1837; it was the rumour that the Indians, trading with the Russians in Alaska, might attack. In other words, "the cold war, *circa* 1837."

It would be ludicrous to compare our modes of transport; he by foot and canoe, and we in a plane and driving a Land-Rover over the well graded Alaska and Cassiar-Stewart Highways. But we and Robert Campbell had one thing in common; we were both bound for the Stikine, he to determine whether or not the river's upper reaches were the Stikine or the Pelly, while we wanted just to visit this remote river which has seen so much of British Columbia's history.

In 1833 Chief Trader J. M. McLeod of the Hudson's Bay Company discovered Dease Lake, and three years later, a certain Mr. Hutchinson, in charge of Fort Halkett, beside today's Alaska Highway, was ordered to establish a trading post there and generally to explore the area.

Hutchinson's expedition set forth in high spirits, but they had not gone far when, as Robert Campbell later noted in his Journal, "an alarm was up that hundreds of Russian-Indians were advancing on the camp to murder them all."

Campbell recorded that a panic seized the whole party and they ran pell-mell down the river bank, jumped into their canoes and were off, and they didn't stop until they got to Ford Liard, more than a hundred miles away.

The retreat did not please Sir George Simpson, HBC governor, and in March of the following year he commissioned Campbell to fulfill Hutchinson's orders and also to determine once and for all whether the Stikine and what was then known as the Pelly were one and the same river. First of all, Campbell had a job of morale raising to do. His men were scared stiff at the prospects of a massacre at the hands of the Russian-Indians—for this they can't be blamed. But Campbell used some very forceful language, probably a good deal stronger than his Journal conceded, and for good measure threw in some threats about the fate of any who faltered by the wayside. The result was he was able to whip up a certain amount of enthusiasm for the project, and early in March, when the snow lay deep on the ground and travelling conditions were far from their best, he set out to face the reported enemy and to do his duty towards the Great Company.

In July he reached his goal, and on a point of land known today as Sawmill Point he set his men to work building Dease Lake Post.

The site lies about three-quarters of a mile off the Cassiar Highway and to get to it, we had to drive across a small, unbridged stream and along a half-overgrown road, which in itself, played a small role in the drama of the north. During construction of the Alaska Highway and the network of airports and signal stations which grew up with the highway, Sawmill Point was a barge landing where huge amounts of material were transferred onto trucks for the 150-mile haul up a tote road to Watson Lake.

On our first glimpse of Dease Lake, so far removed from civilization, and yet so easy of access now, we thought that here was the quietest place we had ever known. There was hardly a ripple on the 25-mile long lake, and to our great joy, not a mosquito within swatting distance, an event our friends said was worth recording. And so it was easy to sit on a log and forget the cares of life and to let our minds wander back into the dimness of history and see Robert Campbell sitting on a similar log pondering his next step.

And yet, placing ourselves in Campbell's shoes was not easy. Against such natural beauty it was hard to imagine that at this very spot where we sat there had been great human suffering. Campbell's mind must have been full of misgivings as he considered the condition of his men. We felt uncomfortable about eating our lunch here because these hardy men nearly starved to death at Dease Lake Post. Perhaps the very log

73

we were sitting on had, in its younger days, witnessed the scene which was about to unfold for Robert Campbell.

As soon as he had organized construction of the log buildings for his frontier trading post, he set out on the second phase of undertaking, which was to explore the upper reaches of the Stikine.

The thought must have been in the minds of the men who stayed behind, as well as those who set forth into the unknown as to what would happen if, now that the party was divided in half, the Russian-Indians were to attack. It was not a pleasant prospect, but it was a difficult one to put out of their minds.

All went well for several days. To his satisfaction Campbell was able to prove that the river shown on the maps as being the Pelly was actually the upper reaches of the Stikine. Later another river, farther north, would be called the Pelly and would find its place in Canadian history.

But suddenly, the exhilaration of discovery turned to fear. They were now in the Grand Canyon of the Stikine, as terrifying a stretch of water as can be imagined, but even worse, they ran into a party of sixteen Indians. The question arose: "Were they Russian-Indians?"

The men started to run, heedless of the boiling waters below which made a hasty exit impossible. We can, in the next few minutes of this drama, catch a glimpse of Robert Campbell's strong character, for here was the test where the qualities of leadership in a man are tested. How he did it one does not know, but in very short order he calmed and nerved his men to the point where they could squarely face the danger that lay ahead.

Fortunately it developed that these Indians were peaceful. Campbell raised his little flag and made signs that they, too, came in peace. For their part, the natives said they had left their main camp farther downstream to come secretly to meet the white men and warn them that the great chief Shakes would order them killed if he knew they were in the country. These Indians had been told by Shakes that if they ever met white men from the east side of the mountains to be sure and kill them as they were enemies. The report, then, of the massacre scare of 1836 had some grounds for belief, but Campbell told his new-found friends that he was going on, and would meet Shakes face-to-face.

In vain the leader of the Indian band pleaded with Campbell to go no farther. But the fur trader set out towards Shakes' camp. Soon he was in the immense camp and in the presence of the great chief himself. To his surprise and relief Campbell found he was courteously received. The Indian produced a bottle of whiskey and they drank each other's health. However, Campbell's Indian friends didn't trust the old man, and while the trader was in Shakes' tent, they pulled it down so they could see there were no acts of treachery. The meeting between the Russian-Indian chief and the Hudson's Bay Company trader went off pretty well, but Campbell makes it clear in his Journal that neither really trusted the other.

On July 24 Campbell returned to Dease Lake Post and saw that construction was well underway, but that was about all the good news awaiting him. The catch of fish had been hardly large enough to meet current needs, and the hunters, who were unfamiliar with this country, had been unsuccessful in bagging wild life. With the excuse that he must report his findings on the Stikine to the Company, as soon as possible, Campbell set out for Fort Halkett, but actually his real reason was to obtain supplies to keep his fledgling post going for the approaching long winter. In this mission he was unsuccessful, and on October 11, 1838 Robert Campbell returned to Sawmill Point in a gloomy frame of mind.

In his charge were ten men, a family, a clerk and himself. The future looked bleak.

A contact had been made with the Russian-Indians, and nothing untoward had happened, but Campbell was too experienced in handling Indian affairs to let his guard down. Yet he well knew he had to take chances if his little group was to survive a menacing winter.

To keep body and soul together, fisheries were established up and down the lake, and this resulted in his meagre forces being once again scattered. In his Journal he noted that the Russian-Indians kept passing and repassing, keeping them, day and night, in a state of alarm, particularly, he said, as "it was impossible for us all to be together."

The winter of 1838-39 was a fearful one. The slightest movement, no matter how innocent, on the part of the Indians, stirred up memories of the threat of '36.

When the first signs of spring appeared in May, Campbell and his men made plans to leave and head back to the civilized world, that is, to the little clearing at the junction of the Smith and Liard Rivers known as Fort Halkett.

The last day at Dease Lake Post, May 8, 1839, was recorded by Campbell in his Journal in these grim words:

"As we were now ready to start and our snowshoes were of no further use to us, we removed all the netting off, and this, along with our parchment windows, was boiled down to the consistency of glue. The savoury dish thus prepared formed the menu of our last meal before leaving Dease Lake."

Dease Lake Post thus passed out of the ken of history and its buildings withered away. Perhaps, in the end, they were occupied by the Russian-Indians. Nearly 35 years were to pass before Dease Lake was again visited by white men.

A cemetery plot down by Dease Lake in old Laketon.

The court house and jail in Laketon.

Laketon

PERHAPS WHEN the day comes that the tourist "discovers" the Cassiar-Stewart Highway and finds that it is one of the most exciting by-ways in the province, a cairn will be erected on the shores of Dease Lake pointing across the shining blue waters to a tree-covered alluvial fan on which one of the most picturesque ghost towns in B.C. is located.

Laketon, at the mouth of Dease Creek, during the great gold rush of the middle 1870s, and for some years later, was the "capital" of the Cassiar district. Now it stands in lonely decay amidst the forest.

There are only three small craft on the lake, and two of these were in charge of Craigie Hood of the Cassiar Asbestos mine. It was our good fortune to meet him and to learn that he used one of the old buildings as a summer cottage.

And so we piled into the *Janet*, and with a fishing line to port, another to starboard and one to the stern, headed across the lake. Once upon a time, a little screw steamer called the *Lady of the Lake* plied the placid lake. If the stories of her are true our crossing was far more pleasant than her passengers experienced, because the *Lady* was always threatening to blow up. The only panic aboard the *Janet* was when we got a bite, but were outsmarted by this surely immense denizen of the deep.

Late in August, 1873 the steamer *Gussie Telfair*, down from Wrangell, Alaska, called at Victoria, bringing momentous news. The following day the *Colonist*, on August 29, headlined a little story "A Reported New Gold Field Discovered! Is it the Northern Ophir?"

In February of that year, a few miles north of Robert Campbell's old Dease Lake Post, two prospectors, Thibert and McCulloch, made a rich strike on what is now known as Thibert Creek. And then, in July a colourful former Fraser River steamboatman, Captain William Moore, found gold in the gravels of Dease Creek, and from this discovery Laketon began to take form.

As far as newpaper readers on the "outside" were concerned, the birthday of the town was May 14, 1874 with the report in the *Colonist* that "a building has been put up here for a store but there are no goods in it."

Under provincial government contract, Captain Moore built a trail from the Stikine to the head of Dease Lake and miners said that the Cassiar mines "are the easiest mines to get to that have ever been found in B.C."

Captain Moore, or the "Flying Dutchman" as he was sometimes known, was in hot water over this trail, as it was claimed it could have been much better constructed. But Moore was used to criticism, in fact, he thrived on it, and may even have gloried in seeing his name appear in the newspapers as frequently it did. Anyway, by July the trail was open, and so were Laketon's saloons and gambling dens.

"The town is built of canvas," wrote a correspondent to the *Colonist*, "and a few rudely constructed log cabins, composed of three or four saloons where you can get everything at 25c per drink, two restaurants where (if you supply your own meat) they will do the 'grand' and give you what they call a 'square', comprising bacon and beans, bread and coffee, for two dollars."

"There is no public place of amusement; but they have what they call a mad-house, where the dusky Indian maiden shows off her terpsichorean graces to perfection, and where a white man if he behaves himself, has the privilege of going up to the bar and drinking with an

Indian, with the declaration that liberty, equality and fraternity on (*sic*) preferable to the Canadian Indian liquor law.'

Another item in the *Colonist* said: "Gambling is rampant here at present and the streets are literally paved with playing cards. Saloons are doing a flourishing business with the Adelphi (Murphy and Brown, formerly of Victoria) the star saloon of the place and is doing the best business."

(The Adelphi, incidentally, was owned by the same Mike Brown who presided at the Christmas party at Quesnelle Forks).

As winter began to close in, the steamer *Otter* brought to Victoria $200,000 in dust and an intriguing nugget weighing 46¼ ounces which the *Colonist* described as being "shaped like a very large cucumber after a heavy man has stepped on it."

The following spring, in Victoria, a certain Miss Irving was delighting the sophisticated society of the capital city with her concerts. Miss Irving, said the *Colonist* on March 7, 1875 "sang several fine pieces with great brilliancy and effect and was loudly encored." Flushed with success, and bless her heart, Miss Irving decided to go "on tour" to the gold camps and bring refinement to the miners. Few women went into the Cassiar, so Miss Irving was very welcome in Laketon and her concert was a smashing box office success. Her part of the night's take was about $80 and Miss Irving decided to favour the boys with another performance. Alas! One concert had been enough. Too few attended to make the performance worth while, and thrusting aside the time-honoured principle of show biz that "the show must go one", Miss Irving went into a snit and refused to sing to the culture lovers. It took culture a long time to return to the Cassiar, for the boys much preferred Dancing Bill Latham's "mad house" to concert prima donnas.

And now Craigie Hood eased the little *Janet* up to the old Hudson's Bay Company landing at Laketon where he had his waterfront cabin, and we prepared for a feast of Cassiar turkey and Cassiar strawberries the same as we got at the Wake-Up Jake in Barkerville where they were identified as being a "Cariboo" brand. Nevertheless, they taste the same as bacon and beans anywhere.

Craigie's summer home had once been an HBC warehouse and it stands just outside of town. From here it was but a five minute walk through the trees to the first landmark, the overgrown cemetery.

Who was Takachijama, wife of the Indian Coolahan, who died in her 55th year on March 8, 1904 and rests beneath a marble headstone? Or Surian Allexon, a "native of Sweden" who died October 19, 1876? Or "Frank"? Or the nameless ones including the two buried beside the lake away from the confines of the cemetery itself?

There are no answers to these questions, save they were the unlucky ones of the Cassiar. They rest from their labours in the peace of one of the loveliest countrysides in British Columbia.

It appears that no pictures of Laketon in its heyday have come down to us, and so we must reconstruct the past from the venerable remains. But, alas, we do not have the ingredients to give us a complete panoramic view of life in Laketon. As a base we will use the picturesque log jail house (sometimes called Laketon's court house), which is the central building in town, its tiny barred windows peeking myopically at the ruins spread about it; the blacksmith shop, one of the most important businesses in any mining camp, the open stone-lined cellars which in our mind's eye can be saloons or Dancing Bill's terpsichorean palace, the carpenter shop, with rusted saws scattered hither and yon, the neatly walled Chinese gardens up near the river, and nearby, the carefully stacked tailing piles of the mines. These, and the half-dozen or so cabins which stand in various degrees of decay give us the visible tools to work with, and for the other, the human side, we must turn to our best hope, the newspapers of the day.

Here we meet Miss Nellie Cashman, "the angel of the Cassiar" and one of the few women to penetrate this lonely land. It was in the summer of 1874 that Nellie, sometimes known as Nellie Pioche, arrived in Victoria. The sole woman amongst a group of 400 miners fresh from the silver mines of the Pioche country in Utah, she headed north to the Cassiar. Winter, the long, hard, dark winter of the North, had set in when she arrived at Wrangell, Alaska, gateway to the Stikine country, but neither the weather nor the United States Army could hold her back. The American commandant said she must be out of her mind when he learned the Irish girl had set out for the frozen Stikine, and he sent his men up-river to bring her back. But the soldiers, much to their surprise, found Nellie very happy and comfortable, and on top of that, she gave them the best meal they had enjoyed for a long time. A little bit of Irish blarney on her part ended all interference from the United States Army.

Passing through Glenora, Bucks Bar and Telegraph Creek, each having a cluster of several buildings to form what went for a town, then up the Moore trail to avoid the canyon of the Stikine, she finally reached Dease Lake. At Laketon she erected a hotel.

Nellie's hotel venture was a great financial success. And, when fall came, she like most of the others headed south to the pleasanter climes of Victoria. While she sat impatiently waiting for spring to come, Nellie noted construction had begun of St. Joseph's Hospital, and on her return to Cassiar campaigned for funds for the new institution, raising a considerable sum of money.

The following fall, after another successful season in Cassiar, she again returned to Victoria. That winter, the *Colonist* tells us, all that remained in Laketon were "two hotel keepers, three butchers, three miners, four whipsawyers, one teamster, one recorder, besides seven petty larceny poker players wasting their time at four bits limit."

On reaching Wrangell, Nellie heard that a party of miners coming down were suffering from the effects of the dread scurvy and were having a terrible time of it. She immediately set out with medicine and spruce bark to go to their rescue, and for years afterwards, the story of her thoughtfulness and bravery was told at the campfires of the Cassiar. For ever after, Nellie Cashman was the "angel of the Cassiar". She died in January 1925 at the ripe old age of 80 and is buried with so many other pioneers in Ross Bay cemetery in Victoria.

And let us not overlook Mr. Sam Sing, the greatest devil fighter in the Cassiar, and the hundreds of his fellow Celestials who patiently worked the old claims after the white men had given them up. At first these little pig-tailed miners were unwelcome in the Cassiar, and in 1874 this sign was posted on the banks of the Stikine:

NOTICE
Too Jhinermen
Yu are hearby notiefed that iff you gone
into these diggens you will ketch hell.
Sou you had better luk ought or yull smell
powder and brimstone if not hemp.

Of course, the sign made no impression on the Chinese who couldn't read good English, let alone that crude attempt to put the spoken word into writing. They came on anyway, in companies, divided into two sections, the first to work the mines, and the second to grow the food necessary to keep the men in the field. Amongst them was Sam Sing.

An important adjunct to life in Laketon during the early days was the village smithy.

It is not clear into which of the above categories Mr. Sing was best fitted, for he had two callings, working and drinking. The former was the curse of the latter and the latter the curse of the former. It was in the year 1876 that Sam Sing attained the fame which was to win for him immortality.

As a constant habitué of the saloons, Sam was well acquainted with the DT's and the horrible visions which went hand-in-hand with them. In his, Sam saw devils, terrible Chinese devils, who chased him up and down the streets of Laketon and out into the bush where ferocious bears waited to devour him.

One day Sam went to see the Gold Commissioner, J. L. Crimp, about his problem, and suggested that a special licence to shoot the devils on sight might do the trick. The Gold Commissioner agreed that something had to be done. He issued a special permit signed "Daniel O'Connell" and Sam went away a happy man. That evening, everybody in town ducked for cover. Sam was standing in the middle of the street, a gun in one hand and the permit in the other, shooting down Chinese devils left and right, and the bullets ricocheted everywhere.

A few days later, however, the Chinese miners of Laketon were in deep mourning. Their friend Sam Sing had gone to join his illustrious ancestors. Sam was laid out in an expensive coffin, which cost $25, in advance, and a great funeral feast was prepared. On the following morning, when Sam's friends came to nail down the coffin lid, Sam Sing suddenly sat straight up and refused to co-operate by being dead. His friends stared in terrified amazement, and then bolted for the woods screaming Celestial invocations at the top of their lungs as they fled. Sam Sing was suffering one of his most colossal hang-overs, but the commotion, and his condition, didn't disturb him one iota. He lived very handsomely for three days on the food prepared for his funeral.

But never again did the other Chinese speak to him. They said this was not their friend Sam Sing. Sam Sing was dead. And, they added, when he died, the devil took over his body while Sam Sing went to his sweet repose. Therefore, this was not Sam Sing at all, but the devil himself who walked and behaved like Sam.

Anyway, the experience proved too much for Sam—or was it the devil? He took up residence in a cabin about a mile from town. Shortly afterwards it burned down and Sam fled into the woods, and thus passed from the scene the greatest devil fighter in the Cassiar.

Thus the picture unfolds, and just as in Barkerville, the hand of death, and early death at that, rested on the shoulder of every man who toiled in the five-mile long bench diggings of Dease Creek. No claim, whether it be the rich Discovery, Rath, Lyons, Moore, Forest Rose, Three to One, or Cock of the North, was safe from accidents, and the miners had the "eat, drink and be merry for tomorrow we die" philosophy. In this, they were encouraged by the saloon keepers.

They appreciated the gentleness of Nellie Cashman, and she understood them as they understood her, and they apparently tried to beautify the town by laying out a park beside the jail house. But many of the miners, some '49ers from California and '58ers from the Fraser, were as unrefined as the gold they took from the ground. They were Dancing Bill's type, and there was no place for the likes of Miss Irving.

So near, and yet so far, the ghost town of Porter Landing, or Thibert's Landing, on a point across Dease Lake from the Cassiar-Stewart Highway.

Porter Landing, Defot, Centreville, McDame Post and Discovery

A SUDDEN squall on the lake and a heavy rainstorm brought to an end any hopes of going up-lake to the ghost town of Porter Landing, another remnant of the Hudson's Bay Company operations in the B.C. northland.

It lies at the mouth of Thibert Creek and was the supply depot for the diggings of that notable gold-bearing stream in the 1870s onwards. As an HBC post it was of little consequence in the far-reaching empire of the Gentlemen Adventurers of England, and as a mining town, it received little notice in the press. Perhaps, as Thibert's Landing, it did have character of the type usually associated with a gold rush. But in an account in the *Colonist* dated August 29, 1875 we read the town had no dance house "either for revelry or debauchery." However, the account does say that Sam Adler, formerly of Barkerville, kept a saloon and "good liquors" were sold in the two stores in the settlement, Wright & Thompson's and Thibert & Gerkes'.

Thibert's Landing, with or without dance house, reacted with vigour to the news brought down in August 1878 by a French-Canadian by the name of Defot. Twenty-one miles to the northwest he had found a creek, and to prove it was no ordinary creek, he flung down a poke filled with lovely golden nuggets. A new stampede was on, and Thibert's Landing boomed.

Likewise did a new neighbour, Defot, which "appeared as if by magic." Whipsawing went on day and night to cut lumber for new buildings and flumes and an intricate network of wingdams and sluices blocked the valley from top to bottom. The month after Defot made his discovery, the town began to take on the appearance of a real mining camp "with the usual business houses" and, said the *Colonist* on September 13, 1878, "there is a saloon or two." Two stores were in operation, and a dozen mining companies were washing between $30 and $50 a day to the hand.

Any gold is exciting, but Defot's gold was especially interesting due to the size of the nuggets. Two of them weighed 15 ounces and 45 ounces each, and were valued at $240 and $720 apiece. The smaller one was taken down to Victoria and put up for raffle in the Tableau Saloon on Government street with tickets being sold for $2.50 each.

For two years, between 1878 and 1880, Defot showed good returns, and the estimated production was $175,000. In actuality, it was, no doubt, considerably higher.

Now, nearly 75 years after all these events, we stood on the opposite side of Dease Lake, frustrated as a kid in a candy store; we could look, but couldn't touch the goodies, and disappointed we would be unable to meet Porter Landing's sole resident, a Mrs. Asp, an Indian woman who married a Swedish blacksmith and refers to Sweden as "the Old Country."

We now turned our attention to Henry McDame, a coloured miner from the Bahamas, who set out from Laketon in the fall of '74, passed Sawmill Point, Thibert's Landing and journeyed down the Dease River to the junction of a little stream which now bears his name. Up this fast-flowing stream he and his partners found their particular El Dorado. McDame was a '58er, a veteran of the rush to the lower Fraser, and the *Colonist* noted on November 5, 1874 "they have plenty of pay dirt for years to come."

Some 30 miles to the westward a mountain was named after him, and this jagged hulk of serpentine is being whittled away by the Cassiar Asbestos Corporation, whose little townsite of Cassiar rests in the valley of Troutline Creek. During the gold rush Troutline was a placer stream,

Indian house grave in the little cemetery overlooking Centreville.

A handsome hand-fashioned rocking chair lies amongst the debris in the ghost town of Centreville.

but not an important one, although the prospects were good, and McDame Mountain was just one of the many in the vicinity which added to the difficulties of the miners. Modern miners, however, have found a use for McDame Mountain as it contains asbestos, and as a result of the mining activities there, a new era for the Cassiar is emerging.

To the miners on McDame Creek "town" was the village of Centreville, located at the mouth of First North Fork Creek. It lived and died with practically no press notices, and nothing in the way of folklore.

One solitary building remains and on the door, when we visited it in the summer of 1962, was a hastily pencilled note reading "Be Back Shortly." Its fading letters, weathered paper and rusted nails gave every indication it had been written months before. But what is time in this country, anyway, but a mechanical measurement? In the summer months there is scarcely any darkness, and in the winter, practically no sunlight peeps through the trees to relieve the darkness of the long night, for Centreville lies close to the famed land of the midnight sun.

The *Colonist* for April 26, 1876 states "five new saloons" were "amongst the permanent features of the town" on McDame Creek, and it added other buildings were being erected. By 1878 the creek was being worked entirely by the Chinese.

We could not hazard a guess as to what this lone building had been in its youth, but from its size, it is likely it was a building of some importance, perhaps a hotel or a store. On a bench above, beside the highway, is a little cemetery, but there is no indication that it contains the graves of any of the argonauts.

The route to Centreville from Laketon led up the Dease to the mouth of McDame, and from there a road of sorts led to a "town." At the juncture point of the two rivers, a former Cariboo and Omineca expressman by the name of Rufus Sylvester established a store, and the spot became known as Sylvester's Landing. A few years later it was purchased by the Hudson's Bay Company and renamed McDame Post.

Alas, spring and early summer freshets blocked our planned visit to this outpost. A bridge had been washed out, and it is unlikely it will ever be replaced, for McDame has been abandoned, and governments do not usually build or maintain roads and bridges to such places.

One of the pathfinders of the north, Warburton Pike, has left us a description of McDame Post as he saw it about 1892. It is contained in his book *Through the Sub-Arctic Forest*.

"A casual glance at once shows the contrast in appearance of this western trading post as compared with any of the [Hudson's Bay] Company's establishments in the same latitudes on the eastern side of the Rockies. The slovenly log buildings, row of Indian shanties in close proximity to the master's house, and the absence of any attempt at regularity in the positions of the various storehouses, compared unfavourably with the neatly kept forts."

Now a "new" gold rush called our odyssey, and we turned our Land-Rover towards the Alaska Highway, and in a cloud of dust and a shower of stones, we headed for lovely Atlin.

When Atlin emerged during the rush of '98, few people had any idea where this Atlin Lake country was. It didn't take them long to find out. Soon thousands of gold-hungry men were wresting the precious yellow metal from such creeks as Pine, Spruce, Boulder, Wright, Surprise and McKee Creeks, and a fleet of steamers connected it with Caribou Crossing, now known as Carcross, on the narrow-gauge *White Pass* & *Yukon Route* railway.

In all the former gold fields we visited on this tour, none had such magnificent scenery as that abounding around Atlin. No wonder, we thought, as we surveyed the town, that people remained here, for there is little mining activity being carried out now. It is a town of boarded up buildings: a town with a past. On the waterfront, two lake boats, the old sternwheeler *Scotia* and the screw-driven *Tarahne* lie rotting on the ways. And on the main street, a monstrous clock ticks away the minutes and the hours, just as it has since the days of the gold rush.

At high noon, and again in the evening, we dropped into the Kootenay Hotel, enchanted by the sign "Gentlemen" instead of the usual abrupt "Men". On both occasions we were the sole customers. Atlin! what has happened to you in your old age?

Six miles east of Atlin lies the ghost town of Discovery, and enroute we stopped at the pretty little Atlin cemetery to visit the graves of Fritz Miller and Kenny McLaren, the discoverers of the wealth of Pine Creek. Here also lies Paddy Burke, one of the famed bush pilots of the north who was killed in the early '30s north of Watson Lake. His tombstone is topped with the wooden propeller from his ill-fated Junkers aircraft.

Discovery, or Pine City, came into existence in May of 1899, and in August of that eventful year, the Atlin *Claim* said buildings in the

The town clock in Atlin has ticked away the hours ever since gold rush of '98.

The ghost of Atlin's neighbour, Discovery.

new town were in great demand, and most of the miners were living in tents. In the evenings, the *Claim* added, it was a "difficult matter to elbow your way along Main Street from the Irving Hotel to the Pine Tree".

The following spring, C. D. Newton opened the Pioneer Store, opposite the Nugget Hotel, and this store was described in the *Claim* as having "elegant" floors and show windows. Hotels and bars were open day and night, and whenever celebrations were held, such as the Queen's Birthday, Dominion Day or the Fourth of July, they continued well past midnight, for, as the *Claim* explained, the best of watches "are a little uncertain in these latitudes."

Now all is quiet. Newton's "elegant" store, its windows smashed and its floors upheaved and unsteady, stands open to the elements. Other buildings, hopeless in their despair and disrepair add further bleakness to the scene. The Pine Tree Hotel has been moved to Atlin where it is a gas station. "When you come to Discovery take shelter under the Tree" read an advertisement in the *Claim*, back in 1899, and added it boasted the "Finest Liquors" and "Good Stabling".

In its heyday an unbelievable 10,000 persons lived in this gold mining town of weather-beaten buildings, and now there is no one.

The Atlin cemetery, where, under the shaft at the left, sleep Fritz Miller and Kenny McLaren, the discoverers of the wealth of Pine Creek.

Bennett City, a city of tents, during the gold rush to the Klondike in 1898.

Bennett City

THERE WAS one more call to make before bidding the northland *adieu*. And so, back to Carcross, Y.T. to wait for the *White Pass & Yukon Route's* train to Bennett City, one of the key centres during the rush to the Klondyke in '98.

Bennett City stood at the end of the Skagway Trail, and in the words of Yukon historian Pierre Berton it was "the greatest tent city in the world."

"They encircled the lake in a white cloud," he wrote in his *The Klondike Fever*, "the bell tents and the pup tents, the square tents and the round tents, the dog tents and the Army tents, the tiny canvas lean-tos and the huge circus marquees, some of them brand new and some soiled, patched and tattered by the winter storms. There were tents for hot baths and tents for haircuts, tents for mining agents and tents for real estate men; there were tent hotels, tent saloons, tent cafes, tent bakeries, tent post-offices, tent casinos and tent chapels. In between the tents were heaped the familiar paraphernalia of the stampede; sleds stacked vertically against mounds of supplies; crates of food and tinned goods; furniture, sheet-iron stoves, mining equipment and tethered animals—oxen, pigs, goats and chickens. And everywhere, occupying every flat place along the beach, were half-built boats and mounting piles of logs and lumber. Indeed, from the hills above, the lakeshore had the appearance of a vast lumberyard. Planks were stacked like cordwood in towering heaps, or upended in wigwam shapes, or strewn haphazardly like toothpicks among the rocks and stumps. Boats by the thousands, of every size, shape and description, lay bottom up in various stages of construction, most of them still in skeletal form with their gaunt ribs visible."

And they built a church, whose gaunt hollow frame is all that remains of Bennett City. Its spire, with the weather-vane on top, has seen many strange sights.

At Bennett City the north-bound train meets the south-bound, and the traveller, if he foregoes lunch in the station, has about half an hour to spend exploring, just time enough to visit the old church, about a quarter of a mile from the station.

It was in May 1899 that Captain John Irving, the famous Fraser River skipper and coastal steamboat man who was now making a name for himself in the inland waters of the north, delivered what the Bennett *Sun* (later the Whitehorse *Star*) called an "eloquent religious address" at the laying of the cornerstone of the building. The story was headlined "Christianity's Onward March."

Orators don't deliver speeches like Captain John's any more, and it's a pity. They belong to the past, but on that 24th of May, as rough men gathered in the cool air, it was perfectly proper, and eloquence was expected.

"Ladies and Gentlemen," Captain Irving boomed out, "It would seem particularly fitting and appropriate that on this anniversary day of Her Most Gracious Majesty the Queen, ruling over the destinies of the greatest Christian nation and people on all the earth, that away off here, far from the parental home of Christianity, we should at this time be permitted to participate in the laying of a cornerstone to the edifice which will mark another milestone in the progress of Christianity and civilization.

"It would seem all the more appropriate when we stop to consider that here upon the shores of Lake Bennett, at the gateway of the mighty Yukon, where but a few years ago the winds whistled through the canyon and over the summits of the passes with naught save its own dreary sighing to echo back its refrain, may now be heard the

92

*All that remains of old Bennett City is the shell of the First Presbyterian Church,
a short walk from the White Pass & Yukon Route station.*

busy hammer of industry, the progressive hum of energy, and the sound
of the steamboat whistle.

"Yet notwithstanding the eager search for gold, is it not an inspiring
thought that restless man should stop in his career, as did the pilgrims
of old, and seek for a resting place a home dedicated to his God,
that there he might offer up his prayers of devotion and thanks for
his spiritual and temporal preservation?

"What an inspiring thought it is to recall the history and progress
of Presbyterianism, with its millions of sturdy supporters, and one
is even prone to wish that its founder, John Calvin, who for centuries
has rested in his peaceful tomb in the beautiful city of Geneva,
Switzerland, under the shadow of the snow-clad Alps, beside the blue
waters of that beautiful lake, could now at this moment with human
eyes look upon this assemblage and witness on the shore of our own
picturesque lake, shadowed by these mountains in their mantle of white,
the ceremony of laying this cornerstone of the edifice to be constructed

93

to the service of the Divine Master in the same faith of which he was the head.

"While in the providence of the Almighty, nearer and nearer, closer and closer, have been drawn those of sectarian beliefs and denominations, each worshipping the same Father according to the dictates of his own conscience, one cannot but admire that simple, rock-bound faith which through Scottish, English and Irish parentages has been handed down from generation to generation, unshaken in its tenets, unchanged in its belief, with an all-abiding faith in the Almighty, those religious principles and training until the name of Calvin is to be commemorated and perpetuated in these far away Arctic latitudes, and under the lights of the polar sun. It is a most gratifying thought that hand in hand into the frozen regions of the North are entering commerce, civilization and religion wedded in inseparable bonds which no power on earth can break asunder, with the driving of nails and rivets to be heard in the daily walks of life around us; it is an edifying thought that the mind governing the hand which grasps the hammer carries back its owner to the early teachings of his boyhood, and leads to that devotion to Christianity which is in evidence here this evening at the laying of this cornerstone. It is through the instrumentality of such energetic pioneers as our worthy minister, Rev. J. A. Sinclair, whom it has been a pleasure to have known for some time, that brings man closer to man, neighbor closer to neighbor, and he is to be congratulated, my friends, and you are to be congratulated that by this meeting together the present auspicious occasion is afforded.

"We are sure, at least I am sure, that the Queen's 80th anniversary to those who are assembled at the laying of this stone of the First Presbyterian Church, and, in fact, the first church in the rising city of Bennett, will ever mark an epoch in their lives, which I hope will never be blotted from the tablets and pages of memory. For myself, my friends, I can truthfully say that the honour of participating in such an imposing function will ever carry with me a bright spot in a busy life.

"Years hence as man passes through these natural gateways to the North, possibly we may all have passed away, may this edifice stand as a monument of the pioneers who have gone before, the pioneers of Christianity in this wilderness of mountain, lake and stream."

What else can be said of Bennett City?

PART III

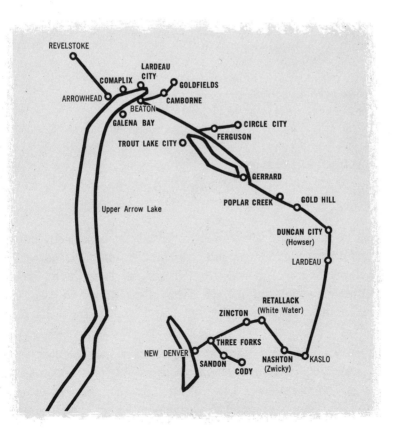

The poor old Minto, saved from destruction by John Nelson, rests in retirement on the beach in front of Nelson's Galena Bay farm.

The Arrow Lakes

BEFORE GOING to Revelstoke, a friend had warned us to be very careful in wandering around town not to stub our toe against the curb and say "damn." If you do, he said, at least three people will appear from nowhere and will pull from their pockets a map showing the level of the waters from the dam. And each map, he added, will be different!

The dam in question was the High Arrow, at the foot of lower Arrow Lake, not far from Castlegar, which forms part of the Columbia River power development. Like Minto City and the "shadowy land of Lyonesse" more than a dozen communities will disappear as the waters of the twin Arrow Lakes rise and back right up to the lower levels of the city of Revelstoke.

Gone will be the farming settlement of Galena Bay, the lower levels of Arrowhead, Beaton and Nakusp; gone will be Burton City, Carrolls Landing, East Arrow Park, Fauquier, Fire Valley, Needles, Edgewater, Broadwater, Renata, Deer Park and Sidmouth.

All these places had one thing in common. They were served by a fleet of steamers, like *Rossland, Kootenay, Trail, Lytton, Illecillewaet, Fawn, Oriole, Bonnington, Nakusp,* and finally, *Minto,* "Queen of the Arrow Lakes" and last of her line. This brings us to a love story, of a kindly old man for the ship of his dreams.

It began back in 1901 when John Nelson of Galena Bay, at the northern end of the Upper Lake, first saw *Minto* chugging up and down the lake, nudging into shore here and there to pick up freight and passengers and saluting the lonely settlers with a cheery blast of the whistle.

For fifty years John Nelson watched her go by, and on April 25, 1954, he sadly arranged a farewell for her at Arrowhead. *Minto,* officials of the Canadian Pacific Railway said, was getting too old for active service.

By arrangement, the "Queen of the Arrow Lakes" was sold to Nakusp for $1 and the local Chamber of Commerce set out to raise money to preserve her. But in two years of hard work they succeeded in amassing only $165, and that didn't even cover the cost of keeping her bilges dry.

Reluctantly, *Minto* was given over to the scrappers, and there was a cry of anguish from John Nelson at Galena Bay.

Before John could come to the rescue the wreckers had her in hand. Her proud sternwheel was removed, the engines were taken out, the brass work ripped out and the tall black and yellow smokestack was torn from her top-deck. Even her nameplate, pinned to the wheelhouse, was gone. She was, in fact, a sorry mess.

John Nelson could no longer bear the agony of seeing his beloved friend being tortured and offered $800 for the little lady. It was a deal: as is where is.

Again at his own expense, John arranged for her to be towed to a quiet little cove at Galena Bay, a stone's throw from his home. The date was July 12, 1956, a date much like a wedding day.

Now that the pair were united, John swung into a round of activities to spruce *Minto* up. From his work bench he turned out a brand new name plate, identical to the old, and from the remains of the old *Bonnington* at Beaton, he salvaged door and window frames. And he put up the flagpole which had been given him back in 1905 by Jean Baptiste, said to have been the first trapper in this part of the country.

"It was a pleasure to do it for the old *Minto*," he said wistfully one day to us, "but then," and a gentle note of sadness crept into his voice as he continued, "I'm the only one in the world who would do it."

John had great plans for *Minto*. He was going to fix up her tiny cabins into miniature museums, and each would be assigned a name, honouring her ports of call.

But *Minto* was not in the proper place. It needed to be moved about fifty feet up onto higher ground, where it could be beached and properly looked after.

And in the spring of 1960 John Nelson got his high water. Sure, it nearly took out part of the city of Trail, endangered the Creston flats with floodwaters, took out bridges and highways, but aside from that, it put *Minto* in exactly the spot he wanted! Who says there isn't a god who looks after lovers?

But high water will come again, and John Nelson's farm will vanish, as will farms up and down the lake, and who will be left to take care of the forlorn little Queen of the Lakes?

Lardeau City and Comaplix

WITH NO store, and not even a gas pump in town, tiny Beaton at the head of the east arm of Upper Arrow Lake has, in its 60-odd (and odd they were) years of life, survived the vicissitudes of a floating population. But luck was running out for Beaton when we landed from MV *Lardeau*, the government ferry, and set up our tent in a mosquito-infested gravel pit.

"If Pot-hole Kellie were in the House," we were told that evening by an old-timer, "this wouldn't have happened, that's for sure!"

Here was that dam subject again.

Amongst J. M. Kellie's accomplishments was the ownership of the Lardeau City townsite, across the lake-arm from Beaton, which at that time was known as Thompson's Landing. The "City", it must be admitted, was one of Pot-hole's lesser accomplishments, for a worse location for a townsite would be hard to find. The town was mostly built on pilings, and it boasted the usual hotel and store. In the middle 1890s all these moved to an up-start called Comaplix, and the site returned to the wilderness, which, in the first place, should never have been disturbed.

Lasting longer than his Lardeau City is the memory of the day Pot-hole Kellie kidnapped the Honourable Premier of British Columbia, an act which, in the long run, was to greatly benefit the whole country-side. But the fact remains, he did kidnap the honourable gentleman.

Back in the decade before the turn of the century, the miners in the Revelstoke district were up in arms regarding the mining laws enacted by Premier John Robson, and it seemed as if there was no hope for the poor but honest prospector. Delegations went to Victoria to present their case. They were kindly received, they took tea in the best places, but all to no avail. The men moaned that the Canadian Pacific Railway was calling the tune, and that the Mining Act, as far as they were concerned, was a hopeless mumbo-jumbo of meaning-less words arranged with a high degree of confusion interspersed with passages of utter chaos.

When, during the election campaign of 1890 Robson went on a speaking tour and spent a few minutes in Revelstoke, Kellie and the executive of the Miners Association of British Columbia decided to kidnap the premier and make him hear their grievances and come to terms. The premier was pursuaded to enter a closed carriage, and literally was "taken for a ride." The tour of Revelstoke lasted just long enough for Robson to miss his train. So far the kidnap plot had worked; now for the ransom.

If, the committee said, the premier would listen to their grievances at a public meeting, they would allow him to catch the next train.

Robson agreed, stipulating that he sit in the hall as an anonymous citizen and listen to their complaints without being introduced. Honest John's ears must have burned as abuse after abuse was piled on him and his government by the irate miners.

Robson listened well to the miners, and at the next session of the

Legislature a new Mining Act was brought down which righted the grievances of the Revelstoke prospectors. As a result, the Revelstoke area swarmed with prospectors, and down on Upper Arrow Lake, Pot-hole Kellie went into the townsite business, and also into the Legislature.

"Few places in West Kootenay, or the interior for that matter, have the natural advantages and great mineral resources of Lardeau City." Thus reads the 1893 *B.C. Directory*.

Not only was his choice of a location wrong, but despite the high falutin' description in the *Directory*, he stirred up some kind of a controversy by naming his creation Lardeau City. A few years after the "City's" decline, the Revelstoke *Herald* on March 24, 1897 took up the cudgels over the name.

"Lardeau, Lardo, Lardeau Creek, Lardo River, Lardo Recording District . . . and to mix the thing up more, the miner's Lardeau is in the Trout Lake district."

"The name Lardeau was given to the river called the Lardo on the map," continued the *Herald*, "and the lake called Trout Lake by an early French-Canadian pioneer prospector in that district. Bye and bye the name of the lake became altered, from the number of Trout in it,

to Trout Lake and two townsites sprung up into a brief existence,
Lardeau on the North Arm of Arrow Lake, and Lardo at the upper
end of Kootenay Lake, near the spot where the Duncan and lower Lardo
(so-called) flow together into the lake. Both townsites being named by
owners anxious to clothe their properties with the prestige which the
known wealth of the Lardeau River would confer on anything even
if only connected with the name.

"To heighten the illusion in the case of Lardeau townsite, a small
affluent flowing into Fish Creek on the west side near the mouth was
named Lardeau Creek. Then, in the division into districts the upper
Lardeau fell to Trout Lake, the lower Lardeau to Ainsworth, and the
Lardeau district had to be content with the townsite. A more careless
and absurd use of the privilege of nomenclature possessed by the
government of a new country has been rarely seen."

"However," the newspaper went on, "writing Lardeau in a red or
black ink on a map cannot in the nature of things prove of any
particular permanent benefit to the localities thus honoured. The Great
Northern and Silver Cup and other well known Lardeau leads are still
to be found where nature put them on the banks of the original Lardeau
River, and the rising townsites of Lardeau or Lardo have reverted to

their original obscurity as part of the primeval wilderness. This being the case there seems to be no necessity to perpetuate this multiplication, since there is nobody with the slightest interest in keeping it up. The townsites of Lardeau and Lardo can disappear from the map altogether with Lardeau Creek, and the real Lardeau river receives its proper title as the Upper Lardeau above Trout Lake and the Lower Lardeau with it, while that grotesque absurdity "Lardo" can be consigned to oblivion altogether.

"Then if the Lardeau recording district, which, as we have shown, is outside of the real Lardeau mining country altogether, received the name of the Fish Creek district, from the section traversed by that creek in and near which most of the principal discoveries have so far been made, the official map of the Kootenay would be cleared of a great deal of totally unnecessary and wholly nonsensical mystification."

At least part of the problem was solved by a wealthy Englishman named Hewett Bostock, later to be a senator and Speaker of the Honourable Senate. He established a sawmill a couple of miles down the lake, laid out the townsite of Comaplix and thereby wrote *finis* to Pot-hole Kellie's Lardeau City. In fact the City packed up and moved *en masse*, including Magee and Green's Lardeau Hotel, which at the new location was doubled in size.

What Lardeau City lacked, Comaplix had. People from Revelstoke used to board the little steamer *Revelstoke* for picnics down at the mill, and for nearly 20 years Comaplix prospered, turning out millions of board feet of lumber and acting as a jumping off place for the mineral laden hills in the vicinity. Regular steamboat service was maintained by the company, utilizing the little steamers *Archer* and *Lardeau* between Arrowhead, the end of steel of a CPR branchline and Comaplix.

Early in April, 1915, when ice still covered the lake, fire broke out in three or four places in town, and it was said the blaze was of incendiary origin. The Vancouver *Province* noted "no strangers were in Comaplix that day."

Practically the whole of Comaplix was destroyed, except for the school and a few small houses. The steamer *Revelstoke*, which wintered at Comaplix, was unable to escape. Her sternwheel lies rotting on the beach and this, with piles of sawdust covering the overgrown ground, are all that remain of what was once the busiest sawmill town in the interior.

Camborne in the days of yore.

Camborne and Goldfields

THE VERY WORD "gold" can easily cast a spell over a man, and he'll go in search of it, even if he hasn't the faintest idea what the stuff looks like. Sometimes all he'll find is "fool's gold" but until his "gold" is disproved, he's a happy man.

In the spring of 1899 several New Brunswickers, working for the Kootenay Lumber Company at Comaplix, began to take an interest in the comings and goings of prospectors up the nearby Incomappleux River. One of them was James W. Tweedie, who remarked to a friend that he "didn't believe there was such a devil of a lot of science about prospecting, all you have to do," he said, "is to go out and poke around a bit, and if you find something, then you're a good prospector, and if you don't find anything, then you're no good."

Ah, sweet innocence!

To prove his point, Tweedie, along with another man by the name of Boudrie, set out and shortly afterwards staked the Brunswick claim, and later, the fabulous Eva property. Others had examined this ground, but passed it by as being useless. For some reason Tweedie stuck to it, and while doing his required assessment work, came across a good gold showing. And thus began the rush to the Incomappleux, or Fish

Eva mine office, part of "old" Camborne.

Creek as it was sometimes known. (There were, of course, scoffers, and one writer to the Nelson paper said the whole thing was a phoney, and besides, there weren't even fish in Fish Creek!)

Added to the richness of the claims was the availability of water power which offered facilities for cheap mining.

Soon after the rush began, a non-practising Cornish miner by the name of Cory Menhenick who had been recorder at Comaplix, and who knew a good thing when he saw it, arrived on the scene. He was shrewd enough to realize that more money could be made out of townsiting than mining, and in this, of course, he was not alone. His contribution to the real estate business was the town of Camborne, named after a place in Cornwall. As a cornerstone for his venture he erected a hotel, dipping into Arthurian legends for the name Pendragon.

Several great mines were located close to the camp, the best being the Eva, followed by the Oyster-Criterion (which later merged to become the Meridian) and the Beatrice. Within a short time of the discovery, no fewer than four stamp mills were erected within a radius of five miles, and two, for the Eva and the Oyster-Criterion, were within the limits of the townsite.

One of the curses of the Fish Creek camp was pointed out in a later B.C. Government mining report:

"Unfortunately," it read, "the honest endeavours of a few were unavoidably attended by those of others who were perhaps more interested in making their gains by the sale of properties to the public than in actual mining. This resulted in fictitious boosting, which adversely affected the best interests of mining and made it both difficult to raise money for legitimate propositions and for the prospectors to get either grubstake or encouragement."

Hi-jinks in "old" Camborne days

The ore, raw-hided down for shipment to the smelter from Beaton, contained gold, silver, lead and zinc, but it was gold which was the principal product. In recent years, however, it was the base metals which kept Camborne alive, mainly through the development of the old Spider property, two miles distant, by the Sunshine Lardeau Mines Limited.

The morning after our arrival in Beaton, and after a frightful night of battling hordes of mosquitoes in the gravel pit, we set out for the five-mile drive up Fish Creek to Camborne to visit the sole resident, Archie Oakie, caretaker for the Sunshine Lardeau property after the mine shut down in 1958.

Camborne actually consists of two ghost towns, stemming from the Menhenick and Sunshine Lardeau's short-lived eras. Of the earlier, only the Eva mine manager's house remains as an entity, a delightfully ornate two storey building. And it is even difficult to find vestiges of other buildings in the town that once boasted a half dozen or so hotels,

The ghosts of the "new" Camborne.

a newspaper, and a nearly unlimited supply of "skee", a contraction used when the miners were in too much of a hurry to wet their whistles to take the time to say "whisky."

The second ghost of Camborne consists of a row of brightly painted empty cottages with shining aluminum roofs, identical in design and seemingly out of place in a ghost town. The Sunshine Lardeau's mill, part of which dates back to the glory days of the Eva, and other mine buildings still stand, but the glories of Camborne have gone for ever.

Only memories remain of this town, whose streets were paved with mud and whose main business establishments were not on the right side of temperance, although they did offer sarsaparilla as an alternative to the "beverage of Hell."

The newspaper, the Camborne *Miner*, paid scant attention to the saloons, except reporting the odd case where somebody had worshipped too long at the throne of Bacchus, but it was concerned with the condition of the streets. Once the editor offered the town fathers a bit of good natured advice as to how the situation could best be handled:

"A Miner reporter received today a present of a loaf of bread from the bakery of one Lindsay. It is six inches square and weighs nine pounds. The Townsite Company have been shown this product and are considering the advisability of using it as street pavement, as no macadam they have yet seen has the toughness and wearing qualities of this bread. The specimen is on view at this office."

If the reports are true, the quietest place in town was the Coronation Hotel bar-room, and it was not until years later, when it was being torn down, that the reason was discovered; the walls were lined with quart-size beer bottles which deadened the sound!

For a short time in its infancy, Camborne had a rival, the town of Goldfields, and its arrival was announced in the Ferguson *Eagle* for October 24, 1901.

"One result of the townsite owners not advertising is now to be seen in the Fish Creek camp," wrote Parm Pettipiece, owner-editor of the *Eagle*, "The Camborne people imagined they had a cinch, but never announced it in a newspaper. Now comes G. F. Goldsmith with a rival for Camborne. The new townsite is Goldfields, and if we mistake not there will be more paid publicity than heretofore concerning Camborne. Mr. Goldsmith recently purchased from Roger E. Perry an interest in this townsite and with Mr. Perry will proceed · to slash timber and lay out streets, survey and plot the ground at once. Messrs. Goldsmith and Perry have the making of a splendid townsite at Goldfields, adjoining as it does the famous Camborne group which comes right down to the Camborne limits."

Advertisement in the Ferguson Eagle, November 21, 1901.

Despite this broad hint for advertising on Parm's part, Cory Menhenick didn't rise to the bait, and Goldfields, a mile above Camborne, didn't rise—period. However, a little activity did take place there, and two stores and a hotel, the Northwestern, were opened. It was headquarters for the Northwestern Development Syndicate of Hancock, Michigan, who operated nine claims in the area. Its days were short, and no doubt the fact that the only way to get to Goldfields was through Camborne, with its many swinging doors, hastened its end.

With the demolition of the Coronation Hotel, the end of the road for Cory Menhenick's town had been reached. The next phase was to be far different, for the second Camborne was, by comparison with the old, antiseptic in its cleanliness and temperate to a degree unknown, and unthought of, in earlier times. It lasted six years, from 1952 to 1958, the end coming on May 14 of that year.

And then it became quiet.

Driving back to Beaton we discussed the pros and cons of spending another night in the gravel pit, but before coming to a final decision, dropped into the Beaton Hotel for a quick beer. More dam maps were produced, and we had the distinct feeling that not only were the Arrow Lakes to be dammed but so was the government.

"Say," cried a voice from somewhere, "are you fellows going to Trout Lake? Better hurry, for they're going to 'blow the road' in an hour and it'll be closed for 48 hours!"

The "gravel pit crisis" was over, and an Arab would have been impressed by the celerity with which we folded our tent and stole away.

When the mines boomed, Ferguson boomed. When they closed, Ferguson closed.

Trout Lake City, Ferguson and Circle City

FERGUSON AND Trout Lake City, only seven miles apart, were rivals, although when it came down to hard, cold facts, neither could get along without the other. Circle City, "the coming Butte of the Trout Lake country", as the advertisements said, was, on the other hand, a dream which turned into a joke—and a bad one at that.

It was more than just the altitude that made Ferguson look down on the city by the lake. It had begun with the lofty name St. David's, rather more than adequately complimenting its founder, David Ferguson, and it was here that the mines were located, notably, the Triune, Silver Cup, Nettie L. and the Great Northern, and it could truthfully boast that "Ferguson was the money-making place."

Trout Lake, the supply base for the "money place" claimed the honours of "social center" of the Lardeau district, but even this claim could be refuted, and this was frequently done, especially by the fiery editor of the Ferguson *Eagle*. His opposition was J. L. Langstaff of the Trout Lake *Topic*, who printed his first issue on silk.

109

Andy Daney's six horse team on the road between Ferguson and Trout Lake City.

By 1900, five years after David Ferguson pre-empted his townsite, both places had a population of about 1000 souls. A wagon road had been built three years before, linking the two communities with Thompson's Landing, which, later, because of confusion between it and Trout Lake over the initials "T.L." on freight bills, became Beaton. In 1902 the C.P.R. put a steamer on the lake to link Trout Lake City with Gerrard, the terminus of their Lardeau branch.

These are all significant dates in the story of the two cities of· the Lardeau, but for the visitor today, the year 1897 stands out as being more dramatic. For in that year the Lardeau Hotel at Ferguson opened its doors for business, and down in Trout Lake, Mrs. Alice Jowett went into the hotel business.

Ferguson had nearly all the qualities needed to be the perfect ghost town when we visited it in the summer of 1960. It had an aging, forlorn hotel, which under the managership of a young couple, the grand-children of the original owner, was desperately trying to make a comeback; a

110

jail house, with the iron bars still in place, but, good heavens, it had pink lace curtains in the windows; the venerable Imperial Bank building, a community hall with a tuneless piano, and most important of all, a genial couple who had lived in Ferguson for 60 years, through good times and bad, the Daneys.

When Andy Daney died in January, 1963 in Vancouver at the age of 93, his obituary writer described him as a "packer extraordinary." Few people in the country knew him by his given names, Seldon Morton Daney, but they could tell incredible stories of his 100-horse trains moving heavy steel cables up tortuous mountain trails high above Ferguson. Everybody who visited the Daneys was made welcome, and on the afternoon we dropped in, countless pots of fresh tea were brewed, and Mrs. Daney's eyes sparkled when she talked of Ferguson's boom days, and displayed her collection of heavy nuggets.

"Wouldn't you just like to know where I got them, honey?" she asked and then added, "I'm sure your wife won't mind me calling you 'honey'. After all, honey, I'm over 80."

Of course we wanted to know where she got those beautiful nuggets, but the look in her eye and the tone of her voice indicated it was her tantalizing secret, one to be savoured and to tease others with.

On November 21, 1900 the Ferguson *Eagle* had announced a wedding between Miss Eveline Jowett, daughter of Mrs. Alice Jowett of Trout

Advertisement in the Ferguson Eagle, November 21, 1901.

The Lardeau Hotel in Ferguson as it appears today.

One of the solidest buildings in Ferguson is the jail, now a private home.

Lake City and Mr. S. Daney, who had promised his bride the finest house in the Lardeau. On the first of May 1901 the couple moved into the home in which they were to live for more than 60 years.

Mrs. Daney had come into the Lardeau with her mother in the spring of 1896. The Trout Lake *Topic* described Mrs. Jowett as the "most popular restaurant owner in Vancouver" and when she purchased the Trout Lake City Hotel from George Bourke "she transformed (it) from a mining camp saloon into a hotel . . ." Later she was to purchase the Windsor in Trout Lake which she operated for nearly 50 years.

Time whizzed backwards as we listened to Mrs. Daney tell of the good old days, and the tragic days when explosions wracked the mines, and of how "the money from the silver-lead mines of the Lardeau built the Parliament Buildings in Victoria." Life in Ferguson was happy, but perhaps not as idyllic as Colonel Robert Tecumseh Lowery, the brilliant, colourful newspaperman of the Kootenay described it in 1900.

"The residents of this favoured district should be happy. No banks, lawyers, highway robbers, policemen, sheriff, small pox or other infectious diseases."

Some of these came later—excepting highway robbers—but Mrs. Daney never wanted to live anywhere else.

And after tea we "did the town" with this sprightly little lady, dropping into the old Lardeau Hotel (the best $2 a day house in the country, she said) and had another cup of tea, and then, standing on the rather rickety balcony, she pointed to Kings Hotel, Batho's store, the Ferguson Hotel, the Balmoral Hotel, the Windsor, and Hume's magnificent emporium, but alas, they were visible only to her eyes, for all we could see were wide open spaces.

"Sorry, honey," she said, "you should have been here earlier."

Yes, we should have been there earlier, to watch the horse racing down the main street, to go down to Trout Lake on a winter day for skating and to open our coat and let the wind carry us at a break-neck speed of 18 miles an hour, and to go on the community picnics, to Beaton on the 24th of May, to Trout Lake City on July 1, and to entertain at Ferguson on Labour Day. Then there were the Saturday night dances in the hall behind Batho's store, with Professors La Paso and Ahlen supplying the music. If you got drunk, or were disorderly, you were thrown into jail to cool off, just as happened to the man who built the lock-up and became its first customer. Maybe your friends

A view down Victoria Street, Trout Lake City, 1904.

would come to the rescue and pass a bottle through the window, so you'd come out drunker than when you went in.

Of course everyone followed the feud between the editors of the *Eagle* and the *Topic*. Basically, the trouble was political, between left-winger Pettipiece and right-winger Longstaff. The two papers blasted away at each other, suggesting that the other was rather long in verbosity and short in fact. On one occasion Pettipiece turned his guns on the *Topic* with these words:

"The editor of the *Topic* is a great man, a truthful man, a monstrous man, a mining man, a literary man, a man among men. There are none but he. Verily he has a head like unto a pin . . . On and after this date the *Eagle* will not waste one more inch of its valuable space in correcting the erring 'mud hen' published at Trout Lake."

The feud, however, continued unabated to the delight of subscribers to both journals.

"Come back again when you haven't drunk so much tea," Mrs. Daney called as we left Ferguson for Trout Lake, "and I'll show you where the gold is!"

Back in Trout Lake City there was a different atmosphere from the bleakness of Ferguson, for "TLC" shows signs of making a comeback, at least a modest one. It has become a centre for logging operations, and the old Windsor Hotel has taken on a new look to attract the tourist. A coat of paint here and there has spruced up many of the old buildings, at the same time preserving the ghosts of the boisterous mining days. But . . .

No longer does Big Bessie, a huge Negress, dance a hootchie-kootchie on the tables chanting "I's the fust white woman to come through the Crow!" a remark just as meretricious as the Negro marchers in Vancouver during one of the anti-Oriental disturbances of the early 1900's who shouted, "White labour only! White labour only!"

Gone, too, is Mrs. Jowett, she to the place where all good hotel-keepers and prospectors go when their gold pan is turned upside down and the hotel register is shut. If any one person can be singled out as

A view of Victoria Street, Trout Lake City in 1961.

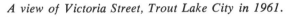

Advertisement in the Ferguson Eagle, November 21, 1901.

representing the spirit of the mining camp, that individual would be Mrs. Jowett. She never gave up hope that the "boys would come back again", and for all the years she operated the Windsor, until 1945, the dining tables were always set, laid with a complete setting of the best silver, and the crispest of linens. And when she wasn't tied down to the hotel, Mrs. Jowett was out in the field prospecting, or attending a mining convention either in the United States or in Canada.

And when she died at the age of 101 in 1955, her ashes were taken up into the Alpine Basin, one of here favourite spots, and were interred beneath a cairn of rocks taken from the claims she owned.

Next door to the Windsor Hotel stands the false-fronted Trout Lake

General Store, formerly the Imperial Bank, which opened in 1901. Its owners are trying to preserve the past with an outdoor museum, and across the street spreads a field with here and there a forlorn fire hydrant, poking its stubby crown above the weeds as though wistfully looking for the miners to return.

Perhaps one of the prospectors who live in the dozen or so houses that remain, will come into town from the wild-flower covered highlands, or the tangled, jungle-like valleys, with news of a big strike, and the faith of Mrs. Jowett, and all the others like her, will be justified.

The time has now come to chronicle the rise and fall of Circle City, described by the *Topic* as "the coming Butte of the Trout Lake country." It occupied a piece of real estate six miles north of Ferguson.

Circle City was born early in 1897 and the *Eagle* tells us that in June of that year Lou Thompson was putting up a hotel there. "He has the rafters up and has already opened a restaurant. His cooking utensils consist of six cups, two frying pans and a reflector."

From time to time there would be other announcements, such as one that appeared on August 1, 1901 that "a mining man" said he planned to put in a $30,000 concentrator at Circle City which would have a daily capacity of 500 tons.

As a result of this announcement, Circle City real estate boomed and lots were sold to buyers from near and far—probably more to those from afar. It is said that part of Circle City was laid-out on a cliff-face, but in the end, it didn't matter whether the lots were on the valley floor, the middle of a lake, or up a cliff; the values were the same.

One day a huge freight wagon rumbled into Trout Lake City from Beaton, carrying a very dignified gentleman, his family, household furnishings and family pets. To one and all in Trout Lake City, he announced that he was the principal owner of Circle City, and left the distinct impression with his listeners that he demanded and must get their respect. With almost an imperial air, he called for a smaller rig, and set out to make a triumphant entry into his new domain.

It was a bitter man who returned humbly to Trout Lake that evening, for his arrival in Circle City had exactly doubled the population.

Circle City was to have been a port of call on this odyssey, but two weeks before our arrival in Ferguson, Lou Thompson's "hotel"—actually nothing more than a shack—burned down and so there was nothing left at Circle City.

117

The untidy ruins of Gerrard, terminus of the Arrowhead & Kootenay Railway.

Gerrard, Poplar Creek and Goldhill

THE HEADING of this section reads like the call-board on a railway platform, and it could have been, for all these points were stations on the *Arrowhead & Kootenay Railway*, better known as the Lardeau branch of the CPR. Like the towns it served from 1900 until the Second World War, it is a ghost, "defunct" in the words of an act of Parliament, and its right-of-way is now a road.

Despite its title, it never got as far as Arrowhead, but only to the eastern shore of Trout Lake where round-houses and other railway paraphernalia were erected at Gerrard. It took some time for Gerrard to evolve as a name on the map, for it appears as Selkirk City, Twin Falls and Duchesney, before the railway company selected a name to honor a Kaslo bank manager. (Surely, said the *Eagle*, the CPR, if they care anything for the interests of Trout Lake, will also change the name of that rising town.)

Construction of the railway out from Lardeau began in July 1899 and the *Topic* said "six new hotels will be built during the next thirty days" at Selkirk. Louis Morigeau, a descendent of the first family to take up residence in the East Kootenay, who ran a trap-line at the end of the lake told the *Eagle* that he thought Selkirk had "great possibilities before it."

"It is surrounded by good mineral claims." said the *Eagle*. "There is unlimited water power easy of access for smelting purposes, the CPR are

118

interested in the town and has many attractive reasons why it should make a rising city with the construction of the CPR to that point . . . "

Gerrard grew with the mines and died with the mines of the Trout Lake-Ferguson district, but it was not strictly a mining town. From here a thrice-a-week steamboat schedule was maintained on Trout Lake, and an equal number of trains ran on the standard gauge rails to Lardeau. In fact, Gerrard was a poor cousin to the up-lake camps. None of the mines in the neighbourhood bore any resemblance to the richness of the upper Lardeau mines, and so, as terminus for the A&K, it is natural that the language of Gerrard was more the lingo of the railway man than the miner. And it is a fact that pounds per inch in a boiler are far less interesting than the price of ounces of gold and silver. But of such was the talk in Gerrard.

In its closing years, Gerrard's little railway became world-famous. Railroad buffs from all over the continent took the stern-wheeler *Moyie* up from Nelson to connect with it at Lardeau. The A&K had the smallest rolling stock of any line in B.C. and few lines in the U.S. could match it.

One of the last trains of the unique Arrowhead & Kootenay Railway.

The engine was a converted truck, the freight cars were about half the normal size, and the passenger cars were open to the air, with the travellers sitting sidewise as the train rattled along the easy grade beside the scenic Lardeau River.

Unlike Trout Lake and Ferguson, Gerrard died a messy death. Its ruins are a jumble of bleached, formless timbers, hardly recognizable as having once been ore loaders and round-houses, part of the life-line of the rich Lardeau district."

One day in the summer of 1903 the A&K leaped into national prominence when gold was discovered beside the right-of-way at a point where Polar Creek enters the Lardeau River. A stampede ensued, and the *Spokesman-Review* in Spokane whipped up enthusiasm by declaring that there was a "hill of gold" at the new diggings. The Kaslo *Kootenaian* said "gold particles (were) sticking out in plain sight all along the lead"

Hanson's Hotel in Poplar Creek, 1961.

and "one can leave the cushions of the passenger coach on the A&K Railway and after a stroll of half a minute be upon the ground claimed by the locators."

By September Colonel O. T. Shaw had a townsite laid out and Poplar Creek, said the *Kootenaian* on October 22, is "thoroughly imbued with the idea of incorporation at once under the Speedy Incorporation of Towns Act and putting in their own water works and electric light plant without the intervention of companies."

"Its growth," the paper continued, "is solid, sound and without the appearance of that detestable disease called boom."

The diggings attracted Colonel Lowery whose Kootenay newspapers ranked amongst the most interesting in Canada. He had them in New Denver, Fernie, Kaslo where he was "Busted By Gosh" and in Vancouver, and now Poplar Creek was added to his string. On December 4, 1903 the first number of his Poplar Creek *Nugget* appeared, and from the pages of this journal we can see these vignettes of life in Poplar:

"A band of ladies from the half world struck camp last week, and ever since the moon has looked like a piece of ruby silver." (*December 4*)

"The Bible is against Poplar. It says to make no haste to get rich." (*December 4*)

The Royal Hotel "has cocktails for the nervous, beer for the delicate, whiskey for the hardy mountaineer and cigars for those who prefer narcotic to alcoholic stimulant." (*January 8*, 1904.)

"A morning bracer is a good thing for those who require bracing. When you want bracing, brace up to the bar at the Inn Hotel and get a bracer that will brace." (*March 11*, 1904)

"The church is the only bust business in Poplar. While we support seven saloons not even a parson can negotiate three squares daily. It can be said of the western mining camp: Before the Lord erects a house of prayer, the devil builds a dozen taverns there." (*October 7*, 1904)

One of the rich claims was the Lucky Jack, located two years previously by a man named Buffalo, but, according to the Kaslo *Claim* (Lowery's Kaslo effort) he "did his assessment work above the bluff. He never recorded and his claim became forfeited. When he heard of his ill-luck, he went to Second Crossing [Gold Hill] on Cascade Creek. There he sits panning gold all day, sparing but a moment to his meals and heaping up a great fortune. But men wag their heads and say that Buffalo's mind runs too much on gold."

The Miners Hotel at Gold Hill, torn down in the late 1950s.

"Keep your optics on Gold Hill," advised Colonel Lowery.

If you don't keep your optics on Gold Hill today you'll miss it.

The forest has closed in on the town of Poplar Creek, and its buildings are half-hidden by the thick bush. When we visited it, some of the hotels, like the Royal, recently had been pulled down and only the litter-covered foundations remain. But still standing on the banks of Poplar Creek beside a decaying bridge was Hansens Hotel, sometimes called the Hotel Inn or the Commercial ("the only hotel in town that is plastered," said the Colonel).

The plaster was falling from the ceilings, the walls and part of the roof were gone, and the doors hung at crazy angles when we ventured in. In what the Colonel used to call the "booze foundry" or "wet grocery department", the long wooden bar was in its proper place, and as we stood in need of bracing we braced up to the bar for a bracer that would brace, and pounded for service. A meek little mouse scurried across the room, a bit more plaster fell from the roof, and all we could say was that the service wasn't as good as it was back in the Colonel's day. Neither was the room service.

Poplar had a "satellite", Gold Hill, and prior to our setting out on the ghost town odyssey our researches had shown there was a wonderful hotel at Gold Hill where you could get a good meal for half a dollar. Such a thing would be a great relief from the mess we created over a camp stove—Lardeau turkey and Lardeau strawberries a la Cariboo or a la Cassiar. So all thoughts were on the Miners Hotel and its owner, Mrs. E. Rear, daughter of John Ulvin who built it in 1904.

"Keep your optics on Gold Hill," wrote the Colonel in December 1903, "It is the coming city at the Second Crossing [of the Lardeau]." By April of the following year a townsite office had been set up in a tent, and several claims, including the Buffalo, were showing high returns. For four years Gold Hill and the surrounding district, including Poplar Creek, rode the crest of prosperity, and then the workings were played out. But the Miners Hotel never shut its doors, although the surrounding buildings collapsed with neglect.

Our researches into Gold Hill, unfortunately, had overlooked one vital fact. The Miners Hotel was gone. Only the foundations remained, and they yielded not even a souvenir. Of Gold Hill, all that stood was a chicken house and a rather curious little building off by itself which resembled a sentry box in front of Buckingham Palace, only this particular one could have housed two Guardsmen quite comfortably.

Duncan City and Howser

DUNCAN LAKE, just north of Kootenay Lake, and connected with it by the Duncan River, bears a proud name, one reaching back to the days of David Thompson, the great map-maker for the North West Company, the Montreal-based rival of the Hudson's Bay Company. He named the Duncan Range of mountains after Duncan McGillivray, one of the partners and agents of the fur concern, and presumably Duncan Lake takes its name from the magnificent range of high, snow-capped peaks.

Once upon a time, a few years after placer gold was discovered in the upper reaches of Duncan Lake, in 1891, there came into existence a town called Duncan City. It called itself the "supply town of the Lardo-Duncan district" and it is said that at one time there were 20 hotels there.

We discussed this city of the past with Billy Clark of Howser, who had been there since 1903, and he took us out on the road in front of his neat lake-side cottage and pointed to a wooded benchland about a hundred yards away.

"Duncan City—there it is. All bawdy houses, hotels, saloons and two Chinese laundries!"

By the time Billy arrived in Howser, Duncan City had long since gone into its decline, for its life-span was less than a decade. And now the site of Duncan City, and lovely Howser itself, was doomed to disappear behind the Duncan Lake storage dam, another part of the great Columbia River hydro-development scheme.

At one time, Billy told us, Howser was really going places. Two railways, the *Canadian Pacific* and the *Great Northern*, built lines up from Lardeau, but neither ever put a train into service. Steamboats called in *en route* to Hailey's Landing and other up-lake points, and perhaps 5000 men passed through on their way to the diggings. When the mines were played out, Howser became a fruit ranching centre, and the home of the much-maligned "remittance man" whose bad traits, and not the many good ones so often possessed, are so well remembered.

These, however, are not the things by which Howser will be remembered when the waters rise and the little community passes out of existence. No, it will be Red McLeod, the "immortal horse thief".

Time has erased from the ken of man McLeod's Christian name, but it will never erase his memory. He did nothing, absolutely nothing, to better the welfare of his fellow man. He hated toil of any kind, and yet worked hard at his chosen profession. He had no roots to cling to, and nearly every mining camp in the East and West Kootenay knew him, as did every rancher, and *they* knew him well. Billy Clark knew him too, and said he was a big heavy man with flaming red hair, and remarked that Red was a likeable enough fellow, but not one you would bring home for Sunday dinner.

Red got himself involved in a couple of hotel shooting scrapes at nearby Argenta and almost left this world; instead he got himself in trouble with the law. The law was a ponderous thing, something to be upheld in the spring and summer months when the climate of the Kootenay was at its best. But when the first signs of fall and the approaching winter could be felt in the air, Red relaxed a bit and allowed himself to be arrested and be put up for the winter in a warm, comfortable jail.

Horses were his weak point, and one day, down in Nelson, he "borrowed" a team of horses from a barn and sold them for $300. Later that night Red re-stole them and returned the team to their original owner. McLeod could never understand human nature, for neither party, including the man who got his own team back, was amused, and Red went to jail for three months. It was this insatiable love for horse flesh that brought him immortality.

One day he was caught over in the East Kootenay riding a horse the police had good reason to believe was not his. It was summertime, and certainly not the season of the year to spend behind bars. Enroute down to Fort Steele where he was to face the majesty of the law, Red and his police escort stopped for a drink beside a little stream which flows into the Kootenay River. Suddenly, Red leaped on his horse and charged across the creek and up a hill. As he vanished into the woods, he called down "Ta-ta!" to the flabbergasted policeman.

This creek is now known as Ta-Ta Creek, and there is a post office of that name in the vicinity. Thus did Red McLeod, who lies buried in the Kaslo cemetery, earn his perpetual fame.

Red knew Duncan City in its prime, and it was that place we now set out to explore. At least, as far as the saloons were concerned, Billy Clark's description stands up. Duncan City today is nothing more than a great pile of empty, oblong 40-ounce whisky bottles, an interior decorator's dream.

The townsite is now owned by Hans Rasmussen, a strange man, with tastes so out of place here at the fringe of civilization. For here on the site of Duncan City we drank delicious imported ale, and nibbled on fine cheeses which he himself had blended, inspected a wine cellar stocked with vintages fit for a connoisseur, and we shattered part of the Seventh Commandment as we fingered the hand-made pipes in his pipe rack and sniffed the aroma of rare imported tobaccos.

And, after having been in some of the filthiest shacks imaginable just before coming to Howser, to see floors, walls and furniture polished so you could practically use them as shaving mirrors, made Duncan City's reputation seem unreal.

Nashton, Retallack and Zincton

"SILVER, LEAD and hell are raised in the Slocan and unless you can take a hand in producing these articles your services are not required."

Thus spake Colonel Lowery, and after bidding farewell to SS *Moyie*, sister ship to the battered *Minto*, and now a museum in Kaslo, we left Kaslo and headed west to the silvery Slocan.

Today little silver and little lead is raised in the Slocan, and for that matter, there is small opportunity to raise hell. As it is, the road to New Denver is lined with ghost towns, and even the road itself, in part, is the ghost of a railway, the turbulent *Kaslo & Slocan*.

The K&S, with its little wood-burning engines, climbed the steep grades daily on the 22-mile line run to Sandon, charging passengers a mere seven cents a mile, but freight was different. That was a matter of getting all the traffic would bear. It was built in 1895, and in 1900 was taken over by the *Great Northern*, only to be abandoned by them in 1910. For two years it was operated by a committee of Kaslo residents, and in 1912 it was taken over by the *CPR*.

In the late 1880s, before the days of Kaslo, Ainsworth, down-lake toward Nelson, was the key point in the West Kootenay. To Ainsworth a prospector named Jim Brennan brought some samples which assayed as

A pretty little ghost town, Nashton was a shipping center for such mines as the Cork-Province and other properties up Kane Creek.

high as 150 ounces of silver to the ton, and a rush to the new mining area resulted. From it Kaslo and the Slocan came into their own.

Then came the month of September, 1891, and the ninth day. A former circus performer turned miner, Eli Carpenter and John L. (Jack) Seaton climbed Payne Mountain to the north of present-day Sandon in the hopes of observing a more direct route back to Ainsworth. On the summit they discovered outcroppings of the Payne vein and staked a claim on it. The story is told that on their return to Ainsworth, Carpenter deceived Seaton by showing him assay returns from another property instead of the rich values from the Payne samples.

Seaton immediately lost interest in the discovery until Charles Olsen, the owner of a hotel at Ainsworth, happened to overhear Carpenter planning with another man to return to the Payne and stake all surrounding ground. Seaton, it seemed, was to be left out in the cold.

Olsen subsequently persuaded Seaton to guide a prospecting party to the locality. Carpenter, so as not to attract attention, made his way back via a round-about route while Seaton went directly, up Kaslo Creek, and therefore reached the rich ground first.

The Seaton party included at first W. M. Hennessy, J. G. McGuigan and Frank Flint, but was joined later, near the 15-Mile House, some-times called Sproule's and later, Blaylock, by J. J. Hennessy who was accepted as a fifth member of the party. From now on this group was to be known as the Noble Five, and on September 28, 1891, several claims near Sandon were staked, including the Noble Five group.

The following year, after hundreds, if not thousands had passed up Kaslo Creek towards the new mines, the townsite of Nashton was laid out on the South Fork of Kaslo Creek, now known as Keen Creek, five and a half miles north-west of Kaslo. For five years, Nashton was lying dormant, but in 1897, no fewer than eight companies established operations in the surrounding hills. By the summer of 1897 a large hotel had been built, and several business houses were planning to set up shop.

The chief mines were the Montezuma, and farther up, the Cork-Province, and at a later date, Minnie May's Gibson Mine, subject of much court room litigation in the 1940s. All these shipped their ore through the little town of Nashton, located on the K&S railway.

As a living community, Nashton is no more. Its post office, which was opened in 1915, closed down in 1940, but Nashton has a charm

The town of Whitewater (Retallack) in July, 1898.

Retallack, 1961.

unlike any other ghost town we visited, especially those in the Slocan. The Lardeau ghost towns can best be described as "hotel towns" while those in the Slocan are chiefly "concentrator towns" and there is nothing pleasing to the eye in these.

Thus, Nashton, set in a green meadow across Kaslo Creek from the road, has a charm all its own, and on first glimpse seems to be dotted with little steepled churches. No, they weren't churches, but somebody with a fine aesthetic sense was responsible for Nashton and his artistry seemed to have survived the mines. Perhaps half a dozen buildings still stand (one has a sign reading "Bank of Gopher Gulch, Rubber Cheques Accepted") and some have Dutch doors, probably stables for the horses which brought down the silver, lead, zinc and manganese from the mines. Each building is slightly different in design from the other, and none is harsh or false-fronted.

Nashton was also known as Zwicky (after W. E. Zwicky, a former manager of the old Cork Mine) and 17½ miles from Kaslo we reached another "double name town", Whitewater, or Retallack.

Colonel Lowery presents his image.

THE LEDGE is two dollars a year in advance When not so paid it is $2.50 to parties worthy of credit. Legal advertising 10 cents a nonpariel line first insertion, and 5 cents a line each subsequent insertion. Reading notices 25 cents a line, and commercial advertising graded in prices according to circumstances.

FELLOW PILGRIMS: THE LEDGE is located at New Denver, B. C.; and can be traced to many parts of the earth. It comes to the front every Thursday and has never been raided by the sheriff, snowslided by cheap silver, or subdued by the fear of man. It works for the trail blazer as well as the bay-windowed and champagne-flavored capitalist. It aims to be on the right side of everything and believes that hell should be administered to the wicked in large doses. It has stood the test of time, and an ever-increasing paystreak is proof that it is better to tell the truth, even if the heavens do occasionally hit our smokestack. A chute of job work is worked occasionally for the benefit of humanity and the financier. Come in and see us, but do not pat the bull dog on the cranium, or chase the black cow from our water barrel: one is savage and the other a victim of thirst. One of the noblest works of creation is the man who always pays the printer; he is sure of a bunk in paradise, with thornless roses for a pillow by night, and nothing but gold to look at by day.

R. T. LOWERY, Editor and Financier.

Retallack is a "concentrator ghost", although when it was in its heyday as a shipping centre for the Whitewater mine, the banner operation of the central Slocan, it was a small town in itself.

The Whitewater was located in 1892 by E. H. Kamplan on top of a small cliff. The only sign of mineralization was a little iron stain, but J. C. Eaton sank his prospector's pick into the loose earth and pulled out a piece of galena weighing about 40 pounds. For a mere pittance, Kamplan sold the property, and Eaton took out a fortune.

At one time the village of Whitewater contained seven hotels, stores, sawmill and a powderhouse, and for a time it was locally known as Bell's Camp, after J. W. Bell who established a post office there on St. Patrick's Day 1897. In that year, 12 months after development work began, $240,000 was paid out in dividends.

Four fires, in 1900, 1903, 1910 and 1926 have taken their toll of the original buildings, and all that remains of the early camp is the ruins of the powderhouse. The last operators of the mine, Kootenay Belle Gold Mines Limited, closed down on January 12, 1952.

There is little man-made beauty in Retallack, and even the hills around are scarred with tailing dumps and mine shafts. The empty camp is bleak and uninteresting, consisting of ugly, square, red painted, many-windowed frame buildings which line the main road for perhaps a quarter of a mile.

Zincton, three and a half miles farther west, is no different from Retallack, except its buildings are green and it lies a little distance off the highway.

It owes its life to the nearby Lucky Jim mine, staked in 1912, which at first was far from being lucky. The ore from the mine, largely zinc, proved troublesome to process, but with the development of a workable method to separate the zinc from the other base metals, its success was assured. The mine was notable for the fact that although it was low grade, it could be mined in such great tonnage that over the years it produced millions of dollars worth of ore.

With the closing of the Sheep Creek Gold Mines Limited operation in 1951 full scale operations came to a close.

Half a mile to the westward stood two rival towns which we must mention as a matter of record. They were Bear Lake City and Watson, but both of these were destroyed in the great forest fire of 1894 which swept through the valley, and no trace of them remains.

Bartlett's pack train in Sandon, 1896.

Three Forks, Sandon and Cody

"DESOLATION AT THE FORKS" would make a fair title for a western movie. It makes an ideal description of once busy Three Forks, the shipping centre for the fabulous mines up Carpenter Creek and high in the mountains overlooking deserted Sandon.

From 1893 until about 1921 the town, situated at the forks of Carpenter, Seaton and Kane Creeks, basked in the title "the heart of the Slocan." It had its ups and downs like the rest of the mining camps in the area, but even when times looked bleak and hopeless—which happened many times—it never lost faith in the ultimate future.

The future, however, was unkind, and practically nothing remains of the town of Three Forks now, and this, to the ghost town hunter, is to be sadly lamented. It had the usual conveniences and inconveniences of the mining camp. Along its single, boarded street strode the dandies looking

132

for a fast buck, and the fancy ladies impatiently waiting for the next stage or train up to Sandon. (Others might be seen impatiently waiting for trains out of town, at the same time keeping a watchful eye out for the law.) And, of course, there was the poor but honest miner, his heavy work boots thundering on the board walk.

Trains seemed to run continuously in and out of Three Forks, up the giddy grade carrying empty ore cars, and then they would whizz down at breakneck speed with full carloads of high grade silver, lead and zinc ores. Three Forks could hardly afford a minute to take a breath.

A sign by the road side points the way to Three Forks, but it might as well point to nowhere. All that remains now is the abandoned railway station, its trackless grade before it, and the weathered and time-beaten remains of the ore loaders. Freshets have done the rest, and Three Forks as a community is no more.

In the summer of 1961 our travels led us to Three Forks and to the once proud city of Sandon, four miles up the hill. Alas, Sandon, where fortunes were made and lost during those by-gone boom years, has suffered mightily.

Once Carpenter Creek had flowed beneath the main street, boxed in and controlled by wooden culverts, but in the spring of 1955 these became blocked, and the creek suddenly escaped from its bondage of half a century. A new course was cut, straight through the abandoned city. Buildings fell like match sticks and were swept away as the emancipated creek avenged its captivity. When the flood subsided, Sandon was practically unrecognizable.

Two years before this disaster struck, its founder, Johnnie Harris, died. He and his city were legendary in the Slocan mining district, and when we visited the ruins of the city, his widow was still living there, tied to memories of the past, and dreaming perhaps, of the day when Sandon would rise again.

Harris had followed in the footsteps of the former circus performer, Eli Carpenter, and although he was to make a fortune or two in the mines, he lost all. In 1892 he founded his city, and during the boom years it had 24 hotels, 23 saloons, an opera house, electric power; and men said it was the capital of a rich empire which stretched through the entire Slocan country.

Sandon was unique. Instead of one straight street lined with buildings, it had narrow crooked streets which seemed to dart out in all directions.

Here, mining men from all over the world would jostle one another and discuss the sensational ore shipments which were the talk of the financial world. And they would tell yarns—and lies—about the properties they held, back in the hills.

The hotels had steam heat, electric light and bells to summon bell-hops; hot and cold running water was in each room. Sandon had elegance.

In Johnnie Harris' Reco Hotel, one of the three he owned, there was always the best that money could buy. Solid oak bedsteads, ornate porcelain basins, and beneath the huge aspidistras in the lobby were gleaming brass spittoons. (The ladies might not see them, but the men knew where they were.) In the bar-room, flawless plate glass mirrors reflected the image of silver kings as they made their deals. Other would-be tycoons hung around ore exhibits in the lobby, waiting to pounce on prospective clients. Sandon mining stock was ever in demand, and the promoters knew it. Unless he was careful, the unwary would soon be relieved of his stake.

Out of the Slocan country at the end of each work week a train ran to Spokane, the mining-conscious city of Washington State that capitalized on the mining activity in the Slocan and Kootenay. It bore a roistering set of passengers who drank hard, played poker and "lived-it-up" on the train and in Spokane. Sunday night, on the return trip, the passengers were quiet and subdued, ready mentally, if not physically, to settle down to mining or to the chores of mining camp life.

There was, of course, the inevitable side to Sandon's life which was not particularly elegant. Colonel Lowery mentions it in the Kaslo *Claim* for February 1, 1896:

"Money must be flush in Sandon. One of the Red Curtain sisters in that burg gave a dance last week and realized $250.50 from the sale of 2½ gallons of whisky, 36 bottles of beer, 57 cigars and 8 packages of coffin nails."

There were gamblers, too—some, with long memories, who, it was observed, sat always with back to the wall so they could keep a watchful eye on friend or foe who might come in.

At one time, two railways served Sandon, the *Canadian Pacific* and the *Great Northern,* and the rivalry between the two lines for freight was keen. It began when both lines were pushing their ribbons of steel into the camp—a barn-storming race if there ever was one. Both companies were of the opinion that the first one into Sandon would get all the ore hauling contracts, so the stakes were high. And so, when the *CPR* crews

Three Forks, once an important rail centre, can scarcely be called a ghost town, for freshets and demolition have removed nearly all traces of the once booming town.

Cody in 1961.

The Virginia Block, owned by Sandon's founder, Johnnie Harris, was one of the few buildings to survive the flood of 1955.

won by a hairsbreadth, the *GNR* boys were more than just a little bit annoyed. They were mad. To get even they hooked a line to the little *CPR* station, fixed the other end to a *Great Northern* engine, and pulled it into the river.

Sandon's days of glory were short-lived. Although it had born the brunt of a fire which practically demolished it, and went through the pangs of rebuilding, it could not survive the crushing collapse in the price of silver. Men drifted away, including Johnnie Harris, and the pace of life in Sandon slowed down considerably. But it did not die out. There was always somebody poking around in the hills, or making small ore shipments, and the doors of the Reco were always open to the wayfarer.

Johnnie Harris returned to Sandon in later years and lived to see a new Sandon arise, not born of the mines, but of the misfortunes of war. Following the Japanese attack on Pearl Harbor, Japanese living at the Coast were relocated in the interior of the province, and many of them moved into the old buildings of Sandon.

After the war they moved away, and Sandon, once more, became a ghost town—a curiosity and a tourist attraction in the lovely Slocan

View of Sandon, 1961.

Sandon as it was in its heyday, 1898.

district. Then came Johnnie Harris' death, followed by the catastrophic freshet.

As we surveyed the ruins of what was once the city of Sandon, it was hard to believe the old pictures of the place were true. The buildings which had been jammed so close together, now lay in piles of bleaching debris. The old elegance had crumpled into wreckage. Only two or three buildings remained in the centre of town. One was the City Hall, and another was called The Virginian, probably one of Johnnie Harris' interests, for he was a native of that state. On higher ground, a few old houses hollowly looked down on the scene of devastation below, and they seemed to be waiting in quiet resignation for the hand of fate to strike them down, too.

Before leaving the "silvery Slocan" we made a quick trip farther up Carpenter Creek to the ghost town of Cody, the one-time headquarters for the Noble Five Mining Company.

In the beginning Cody was destined to be something different from most of the other mining camps. Its founders—not promoters, please, —were dreamers. Either that or incredibly naive. Cody, they said, was to prosper without the interference of real estate promoters. It was to be sophisticated. Saloons and houses with red curtains in the window were to be kept either right out, or at the very worst, to a minimum. It didn't work.

As only silver and lead could be raised in Cody, and not Colonel Lowery's third ingredient for success in the Slocan, the services of the Cody townsite were not required. And what was not required withered away. And this was Cody's fate.

PART IV

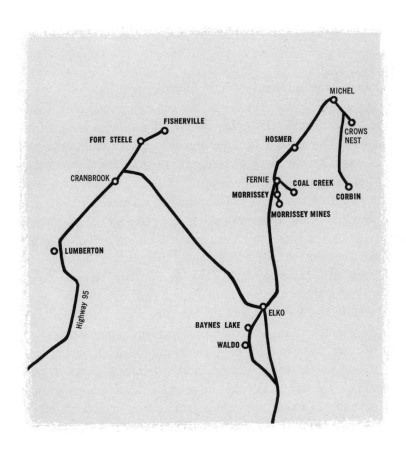

Lumberton, 1961.

Lumberton, Baynes Lake and Waldo

So FAR on this odyssey we have been visiting the fallen mining camps and the trail of "cities" left behind by advancing steel rails. It is now time to look at the shells left by the decline of the forest industry in the East Kootenay. This setback to the economy occurred during the mid-twenties when accessible timber had decreased to such an extent that operations were no longer profitable.

Enroute to Cranbrook, today's commercial centre for the East Kootenay district, several communities are encountered which have seen days of far greater activity than that carried on at present. Although they are not ghost towns in the strict sense of the term, Kitchener, 50 miles southwest of Cranbrook, and Yahk fit into this picture. Before Yahk's decline set in about 1928 the mills had a daily cut of about 100 thousand feet, mostly ties for the CPR. There was a population of 450. Today there is one mill cutting about 20,000 feet, and a population of about 100.

Kitchener had two mills with a total cut of 180 thousand feet per day, and the town consisted of three hotels and beer parlours, two general stores, a garage and homes for the workers. In the late 1920s, according to a government report, the area became almost completely logged off and the mills were forced to close in 1926 and 1930. All that remains today of the business community are an hotel and a store to serve the settlers in the area.

At least they have survived, but not so Lumberton, eight miles south-west of Cranbrook.

An abandoned railway station is about the only clue to be seen from the highway, but a few yards north of the station a road crosses the tracks and the remains of Lumberton come into view.

The town began as Wattsburg in 1903 and was named after A. E. Watts, the first owner of the mill. "Terrible tempered Watts" they called him; and especially when the subject of the CPR was under discussion. When the mill was built, which, incidentally, supplied a considerable portion of the lumber used in Cranbrook's first buildings, the railway company refused to give the mill a station. Watts got mad. He wrote letters. He got madder. The CPR remained adamant. Watts got still madder. It didn't do any good; no station. Finally he packed his bag and went to Ottawa and forced the issue before the Board of Railway Commissioners. He won.

For 19 years Watts reigned over his little town. In 1922 he sold out to a Wisconsin-owned firm, the B.C. Spruce Mills Ltd., who subsequently invested a total of $2,000,000 in the plant. The operation was the largest in the Interior, and during its peak period the daily cut of some 150,000 feet resulted in a monthly payroll of approximately $50,000. A population of 250 was served by a company store, boarding house, recreation hall, garage and post office. There were also modern houses for men with families.

By 1938 most of the accessible timber had disappeared and on September 15 of that year, the mill closed down, and the workers moved on to other mills at the Coast.

Other communities in the Cranbrook area suffered the depletion of the forests. When in 1927 the Staples Lumber Company, cutting a hundred thousand feet a day, moved out of Wycliffe, 10 miles north-west of Cranbrook, the community disappeared. The hotel, general store and homes were either dismantled or abandoned, and Wycliffe exists today in a small way as a stop on the road up to Kimberley.

Similarly, Bull River, 24 miles southeast of Cranbrook has vanished. Its demise came in 1918 when the CPR mill closed, and the two hotels, three stores, two restaurants, post office and homes for 150 were no more. It is now a ranching community.

Once a sawmill town, peaceful Baynes Lake carries on as a small farming centre.

Murder most foul was committed in the Krag Hotel at Waldo back in 1910.

Just before reaching Elko, we left the main highway and headed south towards the ghost towns of Baynes Lake and Waldo. The first time we visited these two former mill towns it was, frankly, by mistake. Subsequently they have become an objective. For this road, and the one which leads to Phillips Canyon are amongst the pleasantest "back road drives" to be found anywhere in the province.

Shortly after the turn of the century, the *Great Northern Railway* built a line up to Canada from Jennings, Montana to tap the Crows Nest Pass coal fields. In British Columbia, this branch of J. J. Hill's steel empire was chartered as the *British Columbia Southern*. As a result of this easy access to rails, the Adolph Lumber Company moved in and set up a 75,000-foot-per-day mill. Some 250 persons made their homes there, and the community had the usual hotel, company store, an independent store, a school and post office. There were also bunk houses and substantial homes for the married men.

These now, are all gone, for the mill closed down in 1923. It was the same old story; the accessible timber had been cut.

Three miles farther on is Waldo, an interesting little community now devoted to farming activities. At one time there were two mills here, the Baker Lumber Company and the Ross Saskatoon Company, which each produced about 75,000 feet a day. It is said that these two operations competed with each other for the largest cut, and this competition resulted in what a government report termed "a worse than average waste of forest resources."

"The effect of rapid depletion," the report continued, "became evident in the '20s and the Ross Saskatoon Company ceased operations in 1923, followed by the Baker Lumber Company on August 31, 1929. It is said that the combined capacity of the two mills was too great for the forest resources of the area and that neither company earned a profit over its period of operation."

The chief building remaining in Waldo is the boarded-up Krag Hotel, whose licensed premises closed shortly before the Second World War. This hotel has a past, and to quote the immortal words of Hamlet, "murder most foul" was committed in the bar-room back in 1910. The bartender, son of the owner, was shot to death by a vengeful former employee. The murderer himself died in a fusillade of bullets 48 hours later.

The Fisherville cemetery above Wild Horse Creek.

Fort Steele, Fort Kootenay and Fisherville

FORT STEELE, of blessed memory, stands on a high benchland over-looking the Kootenay River, once the steamboat highway of the Rocky Mountain trench. Here beauty runs hand in hand with the past, with the jagged peaks of the Rockies in the background blending in with the jack-pines and the venerable buildings which represent the three epochs in the life of Fort Steele.

It was gold, discovered in the autumn of 1863, that brought men to this area. The precious metal was discovered on Wild Horse Creek, which joins the Kootenay just below the Fort, and it was here that Robert L. T. Galbraith built a little store, a building which still stands at the entrance to town. The second phase was the coming of the North West Mounted Police, and the building of their barracks, and thirdly, the discovery of the incredibly rich galena where the city of Kimberley now stands.

The several times we have visited Fort Steele always brought back fond memories of the first. It was a terrifically hot day—Kootenay weather at its best—and the open door of the old Windsor Hotel's "temple of Bacchus" looked particularly inviting. The place was deserted, save for an old man who sat behind the bar reading a newspaper. He wasn't exactly surprised to see us, for Tony, the "unofficial mayor of Fort Steele" had told him there were strangers in town. So he had decided to stick around and see whether we were the "two-up" kind. We were grateful.

The beer parlour originally had been the lobby of the hotel, and on the walls were posters advertising events occurring long ago; First of July horse races, boxing events and other sport attractions, as well as business cards of firms and professional men who had stampeded here when it looked as though Fort Steele was to be the metropolis of the East Kootenay. This role was stolen from it by Cranbrook.

Here was atmosphere, and on our second call for "two-up" we were taken through a doorway and into the old bar room with its long, polished bar, brass rail, and cracked glass mirror behind. The old man "slung" our beer down the polished surface and it stopped right in front of us. Surely, the Windsor Hotel was the last place in B.C. where the ancient and venerable art of beer slinging was practised.

All this, of course, was strictly unofficial, for the Windsor was an anachronism. If it had not been for the pleadings of Tom Uphill, the long-time member of the Legislature for Fernie, the Windsor would have been closed for many a long year. He argued on behalf of the prospectors in the area, and for the traditions of Fort Steele and won, despite the regulations of the Liquor Control Board which called for hotel accommodation as a condition of liquor licensing. Rooms there were not, which was a pity, for we were late getting back to Cranbrook that evening.

Two years later we returned to Fort Steele to find, unhappily, that the Windsor was in the hands of the wreckers. But ere they could complete their work, the provincial government announced plans to make Fort Steele an historic park, and to restore it on the same lines as the Cariboo's Barkerville. At the eleventh hour at least part of the Windsor was saved.

Perhaps the thing to remember most of the rush to Wild Horse Creek, back in 1864, was the extending of the Dewdney Trail from Princeton, in the Similkameen, to the banks of the Kootenay. This was British Columbia's third great road building project, the others being the Harrison-Lillooet road and the Cariboo Road to Barkerville. It roughly

Galbraith's store, built in 1864 at Fort Steele.

corresponds to the southern Trans-Provincial Highway today, and its name is remembered in the smelter city of Trail.

Pushed through in 1865, it was built largely by Chinese labor under the direction of Edgar Dewdney, later to be lieutenant-governor of B.C. In its last dying miles, where it follows its *raison d'etre*, Wild Horse Creek, it can still be quite easily traced, a deeply imbedded track running through fields and into the bush to end at the graveyard of Fisherville.

In these final moments of the trail, it passes by a little pile of debris which marks the site of peripatetic Fort Kootenay, "The Bay" to the miners on Wild Horse. Perhaps some day this historic site will be marked by a cairn, for it is worthy of remembrance. The first Fort Kootenay was built around 1848 by Edward Berland and was located on Tobacco Plains, on the east side of the Kootenay River, about five miles south of the present International Boundary. Soon afterwards it was moved to the west side of the river, and again, a little later, to the mouth of Young Creek. It was also known as Tobacco House. In 1858 it again shifted position, this time to the east bank of the Kootenay about a quarter of a mile north of the boundary, and later that year to the south side of Lake Livermore.

After the boundary survey was completed in 1860 the post was moved to the present site of Gateway, B.C., about 100 yards north of the boundary. In 1864-65, during the gold rush, it was moved to its final location by John Linklater.

Placed in charge of the post was a real man of the frontier, Michael Phillips, fur trader, explorer, Indian agent, and one of the men responsible for the discovery of coal in the Crows Nest Pass.

As the trail continues eastward it passes Phillip's picturesque home—no crude log cabin this—and then melts into the present road, thus losing its identity. At Nigger Flats, where it was joined by the Walla Walla Trail from the States, members of the East Kootenay Historical Society have marked its route as it leaves the present road and climbs over a hill. And soon we were at the cemetery gates, where the argonauts sleep in nameless graves. Around many are the original picket fences, but the headboards are blank with age. This is all that remains of Fisherville, "the Barkerville of the Kootenay."

By the summer of 1864 about a thousand miners had reached this point, and the little town consisted of three restaurants, several stores, a brewery and saloons. Rockers and sluices were in full swing along the four and a half miles of shallow diggings, and the wealth was easily extracted from the ground.

A great many deserted the Cariboo for the new diggings, including the ubiquitous Dancing Bill Latham, but they were all quickly disillusioned. In came, too, the girls; Axe Handle Bertha, Wildcat Jenny, Gunpowder Sue, and that all-round girl Little Lou, who, it was said, was equally adept at pilfering gold pokes, warbling of home and mother, playing poker for high stakes or delivering a powerful camp meetin' sermon.

The correspondent to the Victoria *Chronicle* summed up one of the main problems in the Wild Horse camp in a dispatch in August 1865.

" . . . The miners, almost to a man, grumble greatly about the system of taxation in force here. So far as the Kootenay is concerned, the alteration of the Tariff has done immense harm. For instance, packers bringing goods from Walla Walla pay very high duties under the new Tariff, in addition to which they have to pay $1.50 for each animal every trip they make.

"The Gold Export Duty is considered to be even a greater grievance and without a doubt has had the effect of driving many away that would otherwise not have left.

"The constables here are all on the "qui vive" (I heard of one sitting on the trail all night waiting for a man who he thought was going to leave) but it is of no use; double the number could not properly collect the duty. The country is comparatively open and the smuggler can take his choice of four or five different trails when he wishes to make a break for Uncle Sam's land."

In the pages of the *Cariboo Sentinel*, published at Barkerville, can be seen bitter letters written by those who hit the trail from there to Wild Horse.

"We are without anything to eat except beef and mutton, or I should rather say bones. Some people were fortunate enough to get some oats which they dried on the pan and then ground in a coffee mill. A woman here offered $100 for 10 lbs. of flour. Of salt, tea and coffee, we have had a full supply. There has been no tobacco for weeks at a time, and when it could come in from the HBC it sold at $15 per pound. Rabbits sell for $1.50 and Martens $3 each for food . . . I never want to see the like again in any place or to be shut up all the winter as we have been without a supply of food."

Another disgruntled Cariboo miner wrote: "Here I am in this God-forsaken country . . . Times are dull, in fact dull is no name. There are several Cariboo boys here and without exception they are the poorest set I ever saw . . . "

The Lewiston, Idaho, *Radiator* in August 1865 published a lengthy letter from an American miner which lamented the fact that many of the claims did not pay wages:

"The reputation of the extent and richness of the Kootenay diggings has been greatly over-rated and has caused considerable overstocking of every business. The camp would be capable of maintaining a trade of every description necessary—in fact, according to the vulgar language of California, it would make a first rate one horse camp, but when ten or twelve of every profession has to divide what would be only a fair remuneration for one, it naturally makes the camp one of the poorest.

"Then we must look at the ruinous duties to be paid and the heavy freight charges . . . Numbers of hard working men were leaving every day going to new excitements, most of them having become disgusted with the country and swearing never to prospect anywhere but on the American side. There are few of another nation there than Ireland, in fact I may safely say two thirds are of that nationality. The English officials are very strict, which is a good feature. It is astonishing with what skill and rapidity they ferret out any misdemeanor . . . The Commissioner, Judge [Peter] O'Reilly is a perfect model of a gentleman; likewise Mr. [W.A.G.] Young: and if it were not for their collecting nine dollars for every ounce of gold dust taken out of the mines, would be well thought of. But they cannot help it, they are only public servants; but I believe that one Gold Commissioner and a set of hurdy gurdies would break the city of New York in ten days . . . "

There was a bad element in Wild Horse, made up of men who were not miners, never had been and never would be, but they liked to pretend they were. At the time of the "rush" Montana was cleaning out its

The Northwest Mounted Police at Fort Steele in 1887.

Looking north from the RNWMP barracks up Riverside Avenue in Fort Steele, August, 1898.

The business district at Fort Steele, Riverside Avenue, in August, 1898.

bandits, and gangs like Henry Plummer's, which included Boone Helme, had dangled at the end of a short rope. Vigilante parties roamed the country, sometimes hanging first and then asking questions. Some of the lawless members of society crossed the border and came up to Wild Horse where they pillaged and murdered, creating a reign of terror no other gold camp in British Columbia ever had to endure.

To the depredations of the gunslingers could be added the fear of the Blackfoot Indians who roamed the country and more than one story has come down to us of parties of prospectors being found without scalps.

By the time the Dewdney Trail reached Fisherville in September 1865, a new strike up in the Big Bend country, north of Revelstoke, had called many a miner, and the heavy taxation had sent others packing. Fisherville itself was destroyed by the miners who worked the very ground the town stood on. It was hardly worth the effort.

After the initial rush was over, patient Chinese miners took over, and then came the great hydraulic companies who scoured and tortured Wild Horse Creek, creating a scar on the landscape that never will be healed.

The little log store, built by the Galbraiths at what is now Fort Steele, was witness to these events, and when it was all over, it welcomed the arrival of the North West Mounted Police under the command of Major Sam Steele. The date: July 1887.

Prior to the arrival of the 75 red-coated policemen, Fort Steele, then known as Galbraith's Ferry, or Galbraith's Landing, had been in a state of alarm. Two white men had been murdered up near Brisco, just south of Golden, and a rather unsavory character by the name of Kapula, an Indian, was arrested. This aroused the tension between the whites and the natives, and Chief Isadore began a series of petty annoyances to show his contempt for the law. He ordered several leading white men to get out of the country, and there was great fear that the recently concluded Northwest Rebellion of Louis Riel might break out west of the Rockies. In answer to a plea from the settlers, the North West Mounted Police were called upon for assistance and the men of D Division set out for the trouble spot.

The commanding officer, Major Sam Steele was destined to be one of the great police officers and soldiers of Canada, a man whose word was respected, and obeyed without question. He ordered Kapula and

Isadore brought before him, listened to the evidence, and released the Indian, having become convinced that the crime had been committed by renegade whites. In other aspects of the dispute, a compromise was reached, and the great Indian crisis of the East Kootenay was over.

The Mounties erected eight buildings at Galbraith's as barracks, etc., and stayed there for 13 months. After their departure the people of the district renamed Galbraith's in honor of the man who had "secured peace and order at a critical time." Four members of the contingent are buried in the Fort Steele cemetery, victims of a typhoid epidemic that raged in the camp during the winter of 1887.

On our first visit to Fort Steele two of the old NWMP buildings remained, both badly in need of repair. On our subsequent visit, only one remained, and it was being restored by the Royal Canadian Mounted Police as an historic site. This building is believed to have been the commandant's quarters, while the other had housed the orderly and guard rooms.

The layout of this part of Fort Steele is magnificent. It is just as though an artist had set it up for a painting, for here is one spot where even the most amateur camera fan can't fail to get a beautifully balanced picture.

And north of the barracks, along the main street which was once lined with buildings, stands the Windsor Hotel.

With the development of the North Star and the Sullivan mines at Kimberley, Fort Steele boomed loudly. It was believed the *Crows Nest Pass Railway* would enter the town, affixing it on the map as a railway centre. The population soared to two or three thousand; three churches were erected, a school, government offices, stores and hotels were opened, and the saloons worked 'round the clock. On November 9, 1898 A. B. Grace published the first issue of the Fort Steele *Prospector*, first by a mimeograph process and later by letter-press.

Steamboats made Fort Steele a regular port of call, and great freight wagons rolled through town carrying equipment for the mines as well as other types of supplies.

The first hotel to be rected was the Steele House, operated by Mr. and Mrs. Charles Levett, and this was followed by the Delgardno House, run by R. D. Mathers; the Mountain House, owned by E. J. "Johnny on the Spot" Edson, followed by Harry Rhineman's Venosta House, and the Central, kept by Harry Drew.

The Delgardno, "the only first class hotel in East Kootenay", later became the Windsor. One of the old account books is still in existence, and the names running through it might be a who's who of the East Kootenay. Some of the names entered are obvious forgeries, though. But in its well worn pages runs the name of Ah Wye. Judge not the man by his record in the Windsor Hotel account book, but please do not ask "ah why."

The first entry under his name shows he purchased half a pint of whisky for four bits and two days later, returned to buy a whole bottle for a dollar. Forty-eight hours later, Ah Wye was back with another 50 cents to spend, and two days later, he came back with $1.25—a dollar for a bottle and two bits for a quick one over the bar. There is a lapse of a few days, and then Ah Wye went for broke. He bought a bottle of brandy for $3.50, but two days later, he had returned to his first love, and spent a buck on a pint of whisky. The trial run at the brandy must have excited his taste for exploration, for we now find him spending sixty cents on a bottle of wine. Two days later Ah Wye's name appears again, but this time he spends nine whole dollars for a sack of rice, and not a penny for whisky, wine or brandy. It is suspected by some that he bought the rice to make sake, but for whatever reason, it was the last order recorded to his account, and he vanishes from the scene.

Another habitué was a man who loved to sing *Rule, Britannia!* whenever he got in his cups, and when he died his friends sang the Royal Navy song over his grave. And, there was the Dickensian Mr. Jarley.

In the pages of the *Prospector* can be found a note to "announce through columns of your journal the sudden death of Mrs. Jarley en route to Fort Steele with her choice collection of wax figures. I ask sympathy of the community in my sad bereavement. Say to them I will be with them on the 20th. I will try under the circumstances to make the entertainment as successful as possible."

The note was signed, "New proprietor of the late Mrs. Jarley's choice collection of wax figures."

And there was a P.S.

"Residents of Fort Steele may show their sympathy for me by a full attendance. Please let them not forget that tickets can be had for fifty cents. A liberal patronage will lessen my sorrow a great deal.

Jarley, the bereaved husband of Mrs. Jarley."

Mr. Jarley's grief took a practical turn and the editor of the *Prospector* had his little bit of literary fun.

The abandoned Elk River Colliery at Coal Creek.

Morrissey, Morrissey Mines, Coal Creek and Corbin

IT WAS FORETOLD in legend that, from the very beginning, troubled days lay ahead for the valley of the Elk River and the Crows Nest Pass. Explosions, fires, strikes and depression have all left their marks in the several communities which owe their existence to King Coal, the sovereign-supreme of all that work above and below the ground.

Some lay the blame for the "Crow's" trouble on The Curse of Fernie. In this tale a prospecting party made camp one evening near an Indian encampment, and the young leader of the expedition noted an Indian wearing a necklace of coal. She, however, would not tell him the seam's location, for it was a tribal secret. So, the scoundrel made plans to woo her, and thus learn the secret. Probably if he had spent more time looking around for coal and less in winning the girl, he might have saved the "Crow" a heap of trouble. In time, she loved him and he loved her, and they were married. Her dowry was the secret of the mine. That was all the groom wanted, and away he went to the money-centres to sell his important information to others. The jilted bride's mother, in her

The rolling stock of the Morrissey, Fernie & Michel Railway stands unused and neglected beside the coke ovens in Fernie.

wrath, invoked an unspecified curse on everything the white man had done, or would do, in the future.

The story of the curse does not fit into the historical pattern of eastern British Columbia, and it would be a libel on Michael Phillips, the HBC man who discovered the coal seams, to associate him with the story.

Phillips reported his discovery to his friend William Fernie, who had been a clerk with Edgar Dewdney in the building of his famous trail to Wild Horse Creek. Fernie in turn interested Colonel James Baker, "father of Cranbrook", and at that time a member of the B.C. Legislature. In 1887 Baker and Fernie sent a survey party out from Fort Steele to examine and stake coal limits. It was not until 1897, however, with the formation of the Crow's Nest Pass Coal Company that development of the mines really got underway.

The company, in which the *Great Northern Railway* had a major interest, operated mines at Michel, Coal Creek, Morrissey and Morrissey Mines, and owned the little *Morrissey, Fernie & Michel Railway* which ran from Fernie up to the mines at Coal Creek.

Today's highway into Fernie from Elko rests on the road bed of the former *B.C. Southern*, and where once stood the *Great Northern* station of Swinton, we turned towards the Elk River and the Morrissey picnic site, opposite the *CPR*'s Morrissey station. At one time there were two Morrisseys in the immediate vicinity; Morrissey, sometimes called Carbonado or Tonkin, and Morrissey Mines, about a mile away.

Neither town was a jewel in the crown of the Crow's Nest Pass Coal Company. First of all, Morrissey coal lay at an angle of almost 70 degrees and showed unusual pressure of gas which made development risky and costly. Moreover, Morrissey Mines coal wouldn't coke, so that sealed the community's doom almost immediately.

Back in the bush lies the tell-tale evidence of the mines, mere brick foundations, uninteresting, by no means photogenic, and showing nothing to back up the glowing prediction of the town's future as outlined by the editor of the Morrissey *Miner*:

"There is every reason for shrewd businessmen to locate in Morrissey," he wrote. "There is not a town in British Columbia that offers the business opportunities that will be presented in this place during the next few years. It is bound to be the centre of one of the richest territories in Canada, which will furnish a basis for a great industrial and commercial community. There will be more wage-earners living in and near Morrissey than in any other town in the province, outside the coast cities. Within three to five years there will be from 2000 to 5000 men employed in the mines near the town and other industries that will be located here."

Through the fall of 1902 and into the spring of 1903 the town prospered. It was named after James Morrissey, who, with Michael Phillips and John Ridgway had cut the first trail through the Crow. Hotels, churches and stores were there, and some of the business establishments were branches of those in Fernie. Prosperity seemed just around the corner.

Little thought was given to what we now call "urban development", for just as Morrissey was getting on its feet, a new townsite, Morrissey Mines, began to attract attention, and an exodus from the "old town" began.

A man named Hansen built a three-storey hotel and installed a magnificent oak bar at a cost of $1000. Other hotels sprang up, and, said the *Miner*, "judging from the number of petitions for hotel licences around town this week, there will be no excuse for a man going dry when the new town is started."

Before Hanson could get his hotel completed, company officials had

The colliery at Coal Creek in 1905.

to admit that a terrible blunder had been made; Morrissey coal wouldn't coke. The *raison d'etre* for both towns collapsed.

"With this issue," mourned the editor of the *Miner* in April 1903, " . . . the *Miner* bows its head to the inevitable and gives up the ghost, and another tombstone will be added to the journalistic cemetery of the southeast Kootenay.

"At no time has there been business enough to warrant publication of a paper. In closing down *The Miner* we do it with but few regrets. Our path has not always been strewn with roses, and the hardships and difficulties encountered in an earnest endeavour to get out a readable paper in a town composed of two dozen houses can only be appreciated by those having passed through such an experience."

From the ghosts of the twin Morrisseys, we drove into Fernie and up a draw to Coal Creek and the abandoned Elk River Colliery. When this mine closed down in 1957 the prophets of doom predicted that the city of Fernie would become a ghost town. They reckoned without the people of Fernie, who refused to give up. In fact, it shows no signs of giving up, rather, it seems to be enjoying a mild boom.

Only the silent colliery buildings remain at Coal Creek, the village has been torn down and the tracks of the *Morrissey Fernie & Michel Railway* have been removed.

Coal Creek townsite was built for convenience only. It was ugly, dirty with layers of coal dust everywhere, and in the winter, the sun never touched the lower parts of the valley in which it rested. In the early days it was divided into camps, like French Camp, Welsh Camp, Scotch Camp, English Camp, Italian Camp, etc. On one side of the creek were three churches, Anglican, Roman Catholic and Methodist (later United), and for that reason, this part of town was called the Holy City.

As well as drabness, Coal Creek presented grimness and fear—the fear of a "bump" and the off-schedule wailing of the plant whistle. It happened more often than people liked to recall, and the headstones in the Fernie graveyard testify to the grim toll.

On the night of May 23, 1902, just as the kiddies were being put to bed, an explosion occurred in No. 2 and the adjoining No. 3 mines, and 130 men lost their lives. It was British Columbia's second worst disaster.

"The local details of fear and distress it is utterly impossible to depict," wrote Lew Gordon, the Vancouver *Province* correspondent. "[Fernie] is

The coal town of Hosmer, about 1910.

Once part of a company building, the Hosmer Inn is one of the few buildings remaining in Hosmer.

in a condition of gloom and resounds with the hopeless cries of widows and orphans."

From the neighbouring mining camps came long lines of men, women and children to join the vigil at the mine-head. All night and next day rescue workers toiled feverishly, almost hopelessly, against time to reach the entrapped men. Funeral trains were assembled to take the bodies down to Fernie, but some were so mangled they were taken right to the burial ground.

On the night of the 24th, when normally there would have been gay festivities in Fernie to celebrate Queen Victoria's birthday, nerves were on edge and there was talk of trouble. It stemmed from an injudicious remark by a provincial policeman to the effect that "it was too bad more weren't killed."

The offending policeman was nabbed on the street late that night by a mob and brought to a "vigilante court", and after a "rough and ready trial" was convicted and, as Mr. Gordon wrote, was "rapidly consigned to the oblivion which awaited him in the brush-clad hills fringing town."

The policeman beat "all long distance records in walking" to get to Michel and there, another mob was waiting for him. And after roughly handling him, he was given a flying start to Blairmore where more irate miners awaited him. Again he was beaten up, and escorted to the outskirts of town and sent on his way towards Frank.

For the whole course of its lifetime, Coal Creek lived in fear of No. 2 mine, the "killer mine" as it came to be called. As the month of July 19 came to a close, the sun above took on a blood-red hue, and there was the acrid smell of burning forests everywhere. Hosmer, farther to the east, was threatened with destruction, and there were rumors that the Black Hand of the Mafia had set the blaze to avenge some wrong done to a member in Fernie. At 8 o'clock on the morning of July 31 the killer mine exploded again, and 23 men were entombed with all means of escape cut off.

Anxious crowds gathered once again before the mine, and then a wonderful thing happened. A shout went up from the pit-head—the 23 entombed men walked out! A miracle had happened, and Coal Creek and Fernie gave thanks to Saint Barbara, the patron saint of the miners. Alas, the rejoicing was short-lived.

On the morning of August 1 the forest fire which for days had been sending billows of smoke through the Crow, suddenly got out of control and raced towards Fernie. And that day Fernie caught hell. The city was consumed by flames. Property losses soared to five million dollars. Seven persons are known to have died, and there might have been more whose bodies were never found.

The flames raced up the narrow valley to Coal Creek, and for a time it was feared that this community, too, would perish from the face of the earth. But the miracle was still working for Coal Creek, and the town was saved.

Within the year, part of Coal Creek was destroyed by another fire, and in 1912 six men were killed by a snowslide which demolished the carpenter and electrical shops.

Coal Creek endured all. The martyred Saint Barbara would have understood.

Part of the residential district of Hosmer, the *CPR* coal-town east of Fernie, was destroyed in the great fire of July-August 1908. The blaze could well have been the death blow to the town, as production was just about to get underway. Fortunately, the mine buildings were saved. The sole purpose of the mine was to supply fuel for the great smelter at Trail, and the property was operated by the *Canadian Pacific Railway* Natural Resources Dept. The townsite never had the blessing of the railway company, in fact, it was treated by them with a certain amount of disdain.

The company was operating six sections of coal lands which included 13 coal seams ranging from a thickness of four feet to 30 feet, and their townsite consisted of a general office, mess house, a hospital and about 60 houses "all neatly painted and supplied with water and electric light." The other townsite owned by the Elk Valley Development Company lay "on the other side of the tracks" and had stores, hotels, a red light—pardon, restricted district, an opera house, a newspaper, the Hosmer *Times*, and more residences. Residents of Hosmer were fortunate in that in the pages of the *Times* they could read of more scandals in the royal courts of Europe than they could of the troubles at home.

The mines closed down in July 1914 and the CPR moved out, leaving the Elk Valley Company holding the bag. Company brass said the mine was too costly to operate. Some buildings were removed to Fernie, others to Michel, but most were just torn down or left to rot.

Two buildings survive out of the many. These are the jail — jails seem to be indestructible—and the Hosmer Inn which formerly stood on company ground. This building was cut in half and moved across the tracks to stand beside the highway. Half of it was sent on to Fernie.

As a ghost town, Hosmer was a disappointment, but Corbin, our next stop, was just the opposite. Started about 1908 and operated continuously until 1935 by a Spokane company, Corbin had an eviable safety record. Its coal was free of gas, but not from the menace of forest fires.

In August, that dreaded fire-prone month of 1931, a fire broke out up the Flathead Road from Corbin, jumped from Taylor Mountain to Coal Mountain and started its deadly race up the hillside to the "Big Showing", an open pit mine. Whipped by a wind which was so violent it blew down the *Eastern British Columbia Railway* roundhouse, it reached the Wye, less than three quarters of a mile from town. Down in the valley of the Crow and the Elk the smoke was so dense that headlights had to be used in broad-daylight. Rails were twisted like snakes, and 200 miners fought ceaselessly to bring the fire under control.

The town of Corbin consisted of the Flathead Hotel, several stores,

Roofs are falling in, and buildings lie smashed all around in once-prosperous Corbin.

the largest being the Flathead Trading Company, in addition to the ordinary colliery buildings, consisting of tipple, powerhouse, warehouse, wash-house, executive offices and private dwellings. It was said to be a model town, and certainly it could have been, for it had a magnificent location set in a broad valley through which Michel Creek flowed, and was surrounded by towering snow-capped mountains.

Unfortunately, Corbin died in violence.

In the early spring of 1935 difficulties arose between the Mine Workers Union of Canada and the company over their contract and the men walked off the job. To keep production going, the company, on April 17, re-opened the mines with non-union labor, and the strike erupted into violence.

Some 250 men and women, armed with clubs, hammers and rocks attacked the re-inforced local police, and 11 officers were injured in the wild melee. In support of the miners, 300 Blairmore men set out to march on Corbin to render assistance to their brother miners, but were stopped at the interprovincial border.

Immediately after the outbreak of trouble, Corbin was sealed off from the outside world. Nerves were on edge, but there was no further violence. A week later, the police and the strikers were playing baseball together, with the provincial government mediator, who had had a lot of experience with strikes of all kinds, named as umpire. Diplomatic-ally, the score was never revealed.

On May 7 the company announced they were going to "withdraw from the field permanently," and Corbin's 27 years of life came to a close. Periodically the Big Showing was worked, but Corbin withered away until the town was left in solitude.

Who can say, after all these painful events, whether or not they were inspired by The Curse?

PART V

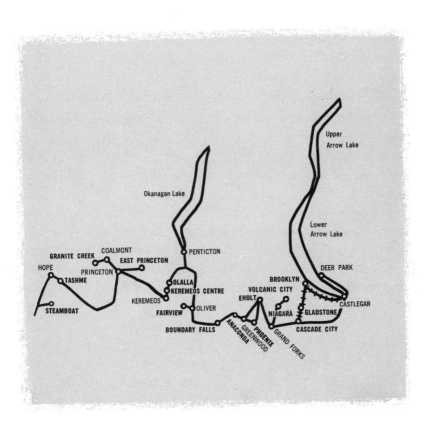

Brooklyn's main street in 1898 featured tree stumps.

Brooklyn, Gladstone and Cascade City

THE YEAR 1898 saw the mad rush for gold to the Klondike, and down along the southern border of British Columbia, in the fringe area between what is known as the West Kootenay and the Boundary country, a railway was snaking its way westward. It was the *Columbia & Western,* originally owned by F. Augustus Heinze, founder of the Trail smelter, but now operated by the *Canadian Pacific Railway.*

And in June of that momentous year, Bill Parker went into the townsite business on the gentle slopes leading down to Lower Arrow Lake, opposite Deer Park. He called his town Brooklyn, and for one year it throbbed with the heavy boots of railway construction men. Now a solitary building and the cemetery are all that remain. Hardly had Brooklyn begun when W. K. Esling started the Brooklyn *News,* a paper which was printed in Trail.

"Brooklyn is going to have something unique in the history of a railroad-mining camp," the *News* reported on July 8, a month after the town came into existence. "Brooklyn is not only the best, but the first in all enterprises. In the new survey on the slope above the business

164

portion of town, lots have been reserved for a Salvation Army barracks. Mr. Parker, the townsite owner, is an enthusiast in this work, and now that the opportunity presents, proposes to give the hundreds of men who are in the camp a taste of religion, pure and simple, and as wholesome as the mountain brook which passes along at its foundation."

Colonel Lowery, in the New Denver *Ledge* on July 23, welcomed Brooklyn in his inimitable fashion:

"Bill Parker came into this country several years ago and staked out a large amount of bad luck. Two years ago he discovered some fine clay opposite Deer Park and pre-empted land around it. The railroad people picked up his ground for their headquarters during construction of the road from Robson to Penticton and Parker called his townsite Brooklyn. The crowd flocked in and changed Parker's name from Bill to 'Mr'. A month ago the shoreline was dotted by a few tents and Parker's original cabin. Now there are ten hotels ready for business with five more building and nearly all lines of business are represented. About a half dozen dwelling houses have red curtains. Schools of black jack and horse poker have been established and sleep is scarce in the town. Brooklyn is swift, but a mushroom. Peterson of Trail opened the first hotel [the Crown Point] and in a short time raked in $3000. Everybody wanted to drink and they lined up to the bar as thick as editors in paradise . . . Brooklyn is a hot town, and only a few of the inhabitants drink water."

The good Colonel might have mentioned the Opera House, owned by Crowley and Reid, whose first presentation was a cyclorama of the Spanish-American War, and the orthodox "larnin' " school with 30 or 40 pupils. Steamboats used to make it a port of call, and down on the wharf was a great sign reading "No Chinese need land." The hour of the boat arrival, like Boat Day in some remote insular colony, was a big moment in the life of Brooklyn, just as the hoarse blast of the steam whistle was to the other communities up and down the twin Arrow Lakes.

As construction proceeded, the population decreased, and finally, by July 1899, only one hotel, the International, remained.

Meanwhile, Gladstone was the "place of the future" and it was likely that "only a few of the inhabitants drink water, " a beverage for which Colonel Lowery had little use—he didn't even need it to shave with.

"Many a young man," he once wrote in the New Denver *Ledge*, "who has drunk the natural beverage at home when it sparkled in the glass, has gone on drinking it until he got a dose of it one day mixed with typhoid germs and became a still corpse. Many a youth, with his face rosy with the hue of health, has gone to sea and the cruel waters have destroyed him. Water? Oh, what a curse it has been to the world. Look at the towns it has washed away. Look how many chairs it has left vacant by the fireside, and the hearts it has clothed in aching sorrow. Verily water is a dreadful thing."

For those wishing a non-alcoholic beverage, the Colonel suggested carrot juice, for he claimed, it was harmless and couldn't be distilled.

By Christmas 1898 Gladstone had four hotels, three stores, and other concerns. There was the Burnt Basin Hotel, the Gladstone, the Victoria and Ennis & Flynn's ("they will treat you right inwardly and outwardly").

Gladstone lasted a bit longer than Brooklyn, for it combined railroading with mining and several interesting properties up in the Burnt Basin kept the town's hopes alive. Today, not even the name Gladstone appears on the maps. Instead it is known as Coryell, and down by the railway station, and back in the underbrush, can be seen a few rotting timbers, all that is left of once-booming Gladstone.

Cascade City, the next stop down the *CPR* line came into being before the railway construction crews arrived. In 1896 it had two buildings, the Pioneer Store and a restaurant, and the man who was to become "the father of Cascade", Aaron Chandler, lived in a tent.

With the approach of the CPR work gangs, Chandler's townsite, close to the Kettle River falls from which the town took its name, began to hum. In November 1898 Messrs Wilcox and O'Reilly published the first edition of the Cascade *Record* and people were saying that "men of wisdom are keeping an eye on Cascade City."

There were 14 hotels in town, and even then, the *Record* said, "getting a room at any of the numerous hotels in Cascade after the last of the daily stages is in is no joke."

As Lowery would have gently put it, some of the houses had red curtains, and the soiled doves who dwelt therein had such lovely names as Scrap Iron Minnie and Rough Lock Nell. The sporting fraternity, that is, the athletes, had a team of "ball twirlers" called the Cascade Giants who, it was claimed, could beat any ball team, anywhere and at any time. It was, alas, not a valid claim, for the *Record's* account of the games often left one in doubt of the team's valour on the diamond. For 50 cents, in the summer of 1899, you could take the family to

Dagan's Klondike-Cuban Musical Moving Picture Entertainment Company's show. And, shades of the Cassiar! There was a Chinese laundryman by the name of Sam Sing!

Great freight wagons rolled up and rumbled through town, past the saloons which never seemed to close, and headed towards the new Grand Forks and the mining camps to the westward. In that direction, townsites were springing up left and right.

"A new town has been staked on the North Fork of the Kettle River, at the foot of Pathfinder Mountain," the *Record* announced on November 19, 1898. "It is called Timville, after Tim Townsend who has put up a log building at that point. The place already has several buildings and is beginning to put on airs."

"A mile and a half north of the new town of Niagara, still another townsite has been surveyed and called Virginia City. It is near some mineral claims, and there is also some heavy railroad work there that will keep a large force in the neighborhood all winter. A two-storey log hotel is already in the course of erection."

The following week the *Record* announced, "A new village called Bannock City has sprung up at the foot of Pathfinder Mountain, near some

A freight team passes through Cascade City in 1898.

The ruins of Cascade City, 1961.

promising claims and several cabins have already been built there." The *Report of the Minister of Mines* for 1899 described Bannock City as "merely a collection of a few cabins . . . but boasting a hotel and bar."

Other towns came into being during the next 12 months, and Cascade City, which had high hopes of being more than just a railway construction town, looked down on these upstarts as something far beneath them. The CPR had announced on January 7, 1899 that a Big Smelter would be built at Cascade with a daily capacity of a thousand tons.

Cascade City's outlook grew even smugger.

"To paraphrase a saying of Solomon, 'Of the making of townsites there is no end'," the *Record* stated editorially on August 26, 1899. "Within a radius of perhaps thirty miles from Cascade the intending investor can have his pick of lots in over a score of townsites, all as it were, destined to be the future Rosslands or Johannesburgs.

"Beginning on the east, there is Melville on the Dewdney Trail, Gladstone near Burnt Basin, English Point, where there is a settlement, Christina City, Minton and Moodeyville, near the foot of Christina Lake (the last two in a semi-moribund state); then comes Cascade and Russell. Continuing west the townsites grow in number, Grand Forks and Columbia, Volcanic City, Niagara, Eholt, Summit, Phoenix, Hartford, New York, Boundary City, Greenwood, Anaconda, Boundary Falls, and Midway follow in rapid succession. There are also Nelson and Carson to say nothing of a few others.

"In case this assortment does not offer variety enough," continued the

Record, "the searcher after bonanzas in reality will find a fresh crop of townsites springing up on the main Kettle and West Fork, as well as further on towards Camp McKinney, Penticton and Hope.

"There seems to be little likelihood of there being a dearth of town-siting promotions for some time to come, as in numerous cases not mentioned land has been staked out with this end in view."

A few of these "promotions," notably Grand Forks, Greenwood, Phoenix and Midway outlived Cascade, for unbeknownst to the citizens of Cascade, their end was fast approaching.

On August 12, 1899 steel reached Cascade City and the *Record* came out with a red letter front page announcing the arrival of the gaily decorated first locomotive. The town went wild with excitement, and a collection was taken up for "refreshments for the labouring men." The sum of $25 was raised, but the newspaper does not tell us what kind of refreshments were served. One can hope that Colonel Lowery was not offended.

Six weeks later disaster struck. On September 30, 1899, a fire raced through town, destroying six hotels and most of the business district. It was suspected that the fires were of an incendiary origin and that insurance inspired the deed. A second fire occurred in 1901 and that ended Cascade City.

During the heyday of Cascade City an English syndicate had built a power house to harness the Kettle River, but, after several years of being a feeding station for the West Kootenay Power & Light Company, it closed in the 1920s.

The *Record*, its advertisements, the life-blood of a newspaper, diminished to practically nothing, signed "30" on July 6, 1901, but bravely affirmed on the back page that Cascade City was "the coming Commercial, Industrial and Mining Center of East Yale."

Mr. Randy Sandner, who with his brother operates a sawmill near the old townsite, took us around Cascade City to show us the sights— and sites they were. Perhaps by carefully sifting through the debris gathered in the foundations that line the grass-covered main street, something of Cascade's past can be recovered. But Cascade City has gone, and only the empty, brick powerhouse down by the river remains.

Curiously, however, the name continues, as the Canadian customs house nearby is known as Cascade City, and despite the passing of so many years, a post office still operates close to the townsite.

Trains at Eholt when Phoenix mines were operating.

Volcanic City, Niagara and Eholt

UP THE North Fork of the Kettle River, beyond the city of Grand Forks, lie the shattered dreams of many mining men and investors. If you poke around a bit, you'll find vestiges of some of the communities mentioned in the pages of the Cascade *Record*, and the two most important of these were Volcanic City and Niagara.

British Columbia has produced few men more colourful than R. A. Brown, alias Sunset Brown, Crazy Brown and Volcanic Brown. Although his story begins earlier, the date we are concerned with at this time is February 22, 1884, the day he reached the Boundary country.

Brown took one look at the country north of where Grand Forks would later rise and was enraptured. He saw a big red-capped mountain which he recognized as being topped with the "iron hat" of the miners, and there, in 1885, he staked out a claim calling it the Volcanic.

His plans for the future were grandiose. He planned to open the mineral wealth of the mountain by a long tunnel and from it, to take out enough ore to pay off the national debt of Canada.

From this great scheme arose Volcanic City, and Brown, with an eye to the future, reserved half of his city for the "hundreds of smelters" that he said would be required to treat the ore. He pictured Volcanic City as the objective point of half a dozen railroads; he proposed to abolish banks and churches, making the people happy and prosperous with oceans of money from government printing presses, and converting the churches into halls of science. He had a prescription for all human ailments, before which would vanish the scourge of tuberculosis, and the medical profession would be without jobs.

It is said that the fame of Volcanic City spread far and wide, and that an American company bonded the Volcanic claims. A company, the Oliver Mining & Smelting Company, with a capital of $20 million, was organized.

But hand in hand with all the high hopes and extravagant words, trouble came marching into town. Mining engineers—cold, scientific men and not dreamers—arrived on the scene and inspected the Volcanic property. Exactly what happened next is hard to learn, but there were two upshots to their visit. In the first place the engineers condemned the property, and secondly Brown took them to court, a step destined to cost him $65,000 when he lost.

With the exception of a tunnel which he drove 515 feet into Volcanic Mountain, that was all the development that took place. Volcanic City never knew the hum of an industrial life.

Brown went on to discover the Sunset Claims near Princeton, which later became the great Copper Mountain mine, and he died in 1936 searching for the legendary lost mine of the Indian murderer Slumach, north of Pitt Lake near New Westminster.

Mr. G. Seymour was, by comparison with Volcanic Brown, a man of few words. His townsite, Niagara, came into existence late in 1898 more as a result of railway construction than mining. By Christmas of '98 there were a dozen hotels, a meat market, and plans for erection of a 300-seat concert hall—in fact, the Cascade *Record* said work had started on the project.

Frequent visitors to Niagara were the railway contractors, the firm of Mann, Foley Bros. & Larson, with J. W. (Jack) Stewart as superintendent. This project marked their entry into the railway history of the

171

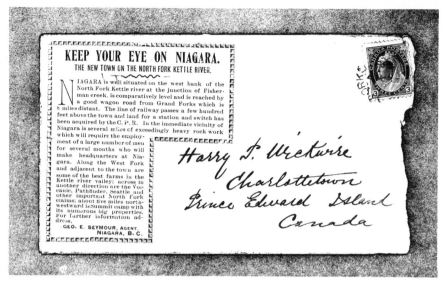

KEEP YOUR EYE ON NIAGARA.
THE NEW TOWN ON THE NORTH FORK KETTLE RIVER.

NIAGARA is well situated on the west bank of the North Fork Kettle river at the junction of Fisherman creek, is comparatively level and is reached by a good wagon road from Grand Forks which is 8 miles distant. The line of railway passes a few hundred feet above the town and land for a station and switch has been acquired by the C. P. R. In the immediate vicinity of Niagara is several miles of exceedingly heavy rock work which will require the employment of a large number of men for several months who will make headquarters at Niagara. Along the West Fork and adjacent to the town are some of the best farms in the Kettle river valley; across in another direction are the Volcanic, Pathfinder, Seattle and other important North Fork claims; about five miles northwestward is Summit camp with its numerous big properties. For further information address,

GEO. E. SEYMOUR, AGENT.
NIAGARA, B. C.

Harry T. Wickwire
Charlottetown
Prince Edward Island
Canada

Promotion envelope of the Niagara townsite company.

province and later, through the firm of Foley, Welch & Stewart, these men were to become involved in the *Pacific Great Eastern Railway* and figure in the politics of British Columbia.

Niagara might have been forgotten when the steel passed through had it not been for what the Vancouver *Province* called, on November 20, 1906, "the most terrible outrage ever perpetrated in the Boundary district."

The day before, in the Canada Hotel, a free for all broke out between Italian and French labourers, and threats were made to blow up the hotel. All that day and into the evening the air was tense in little Niagara, and shortly after dusk the aroused men took to shooting at each other with rifles. Just about midnight there was a terrific explosion and the Canada Hotel seemed to collapse like a playing card house. Two persons were killed in the dynamiting, Louise King, the 18-year-old daughter of the owner, and an unidentified Italian. Nine others were injured.

Prime suspect in the case was Francisco Cedio, or Ciddie, alias Frank Angali Bienblanco, who, his friends said, was in love with the murdered girl. Cedio made his escape from Niagara in a hay wagon and eluded police until February 1908 when he was caught in Salt Lake City and confessed to the crime.

Niagara and Volcanic City were hardly the showpieces of the Boundary.

This distinction went to Phoenix, between Grand Forks and Greenwood, and helping to make the "highest city in Canada" a success was the little community of Eholt, *CPR* headquarters for the hauling out of the ore.

On August 14, 1927, Mr. W. C. Wilson, writing in the Vancouver *Province*, has left us a good description of life in Eholt.

"Eholt was the scene of great activity," he wrote, "as about fifteen locomotives and corresponding train crews tied up there every night.

"A book could be written about the famous characters who composed these crews, about their feats of daring, tests of endurance and devotion to duty. An ordinary person has no conception of the powers of endurance of some human beings, but railroading out of Eholt in the old days tested them to the limit. Crews would be out for days and nights at a stretch, snatch a few hours rest, and then the call boy would be after them again . . .

"Along about '24 o'clock' we will assume the yard was full of cars, loaded ore dumps, empty ore dumps and box cars of coke. The despatcher at Nelson would call up the operator at Eholt and give him the 'lineup' for the following day.

"It would read something like this," Mr. Wilson continued. "Send Extra No. 312 and Extra No. 952, possibly two or three trains, to Phoenix with empties and return with loads of ore, send a couple of trains to Grand Forks with loads of ore, return with empties; send a

Trees press in on the site of Eholt, 1961.

train to Greenwood with ore and coke, return with empties. All trains not on timecard are called 'extras.'

"About 4 a.m. the call boy would start to rouse the crews and by 5 o'clock there would be a pandemonium of men, cars and engines. Did you ever kick over an ant-hill? That is what Eholt looked like in the early morning.

"The system on which one run was operated was called the 'Chain Gang'. The first crew to tie-up would be the first to be called. Little attention was paid to day or night. Trains operated all around the clock.

"The casual tourist had many questions to ask, but the train crews usually had an answer. Here is a sample:

"Tourist: Isn't that a steep hill to Phoenix, and aren't those curves sharp?

"Trainman: The curves are so sharp that the fireman when throwing coal into the firebox often hits the engine in the headlight and the hill is so steep the engine can only take one car of coal at a time. They burn the coal on the way up, then load the car with ore and it comes back by gravity."

"To hear a couple of trainmen conversing at times would sound like Chinook jargon. One afternoon I was sitting in one of the hotels. An engine gave two blasts of the whistle (the signal for departure). One person remarked to another: 'Hogshead is off down the hill, duck soup for the tallow pot.' The engineer, in the jargon of the railwayman was called the 'Hogshead,' while the fireman bore the name 'tallow pot.' He meant the engineer was starting down the hill which would be easy for the fireman."

With the passing of Phoenix's fortunes, Eholt, too, went into decline. The monstrous steam engines were put on other lines, and the hogsheads and tallow pots went, too. The trains of the *CPR's* Kettle Valley branch, now dieselized, pass through with nary a salute to the once busy rail centre, and automobile drivers, racing at 60 m.p.h. or more along the southern Trans-Provincial Highway, pass a forlorn wooden building on the south side of the road and the "CPR-red" station, without realizing that they, like time, have passed Eholt. In summer months the site lies beneath a blanket of white daisies.

From Eholt, the traveller branches off to Phoenix, following in many places the seven percent former railway grade, driving a road paved with iron ore of a reddish yellow hue which blends in a pleasing contrast to the green foliage lining either side of the road.

Phoenix as it was about 1918. Only a few structures still stand.

Phoenix

WHEN THE MINES at Phoenix closed down in 1919 and the population moved away from the highest city in Canada, it was with the hope that, like the mythological bird, the phoenix, the town would rise again and take its place once more as a great mining centre.

The mines have, in recent years, re-opened, at least as far as the old Stemwinder property is concerned, but the city still awaits its rebirth, an event which is hardly likely to occur. Instead, it is the forest which has risen again, and the timid deer wander unmolested through the forest as did their ancestors before the mines were opened up.

Unlike Lardeau City, Cascade City, Duncan City, or the host of other flamboyant imposters which we have met on this odyssey, Phoenix was a genuine city in all respects. It had a well-ordered life, though never prudish, a mayor and council, substantial buildings with Victorian elegance, wealth, and its people knew how to pursue happiness as keenly as did those living in the fly-by-nighters.

One writer has described Phoenix as a "big brassy place, full of locomotives, blasting, four churches, champion hockey teams, 28 saloons, five dance halls, gambling casinos, the biggest plate glass windows in the west and a boarding house where 400 miners once had a fight over a girl."

But how does one reconstruct Phoenix for the mind which never knew it in its days of glory? The visible materials are scarce; a broken stone fireplace, moss-covered ruins, and here and there some steps which lead to nothing, flower beds which have gone wild, a war memorial, a few weather-worn mine buildings, and paths through the woods which once might have served as streets.

And yet, despite these few clues to the past, Phoenix is not the disappointment one would expect. Without seeing buildings, or people, a lot can be learned, and the pulse of old Phoenix can be felt, by following old railway grades until they end in a pile of twisted and broken timbers which once served as trestles over gullies and streams; or, and in this adventure great caution must be used, by inspecting surface workings of the abandoned mines, and the "glory holes" from which the wealth of the Boundary country was exacted. And then, on the road down to Greenwood, pause for a moment at the cemetery, pass through the lych gate, and read the headstones:

In Memory of James McGregor, of Nyanza, N.S., who was killed in the Granby mines, July 17, 1905. Aged 21 years.

Some of the graves are surrounded by neat picket fences or iron rails, and the headstones bear witness to the homelands of those who toiled in the mines: Switzerland, Austria, Italy, Germany, Bohemia, Serbia, the U.S., Great Britain, Canada, etc. And the 15 names inscribed on the neatly kept War Memorial opposite the Stemwinder Mine unite Phoenix with thousands of other communities across the nation whose sons went to war and never came back.

At least a hundred million dollars worth of ore came out of the Phoenix camp, and such great mines as the Old Ironsides, Knobb Hill, Gold Drop, Snowshoe and Curlew, operated by the Granby company; and the Brooklyn, Stemwinder and Idaho, owned by the Dominion Copper Company; and the B.C. Copper Company's Rawhide and Athelstan properties, brought prosperity not only to Phoenix but to the whole of the Boundary country.

The ground was staked in 1891, but it was not until 1895 that the full extent of the immense mineral deposits were realized. Then the boom really began.

From the forest, Greenwood Camp, soon to be known as Phoenix, was born. Log cabins were built, only to be replaced in short order by frame cottages, then came brick homes. In 1896 smelters were erected at Boundary Falls, Greenwood and Grand Forks and the Granby company began to ship ore and the *Canadian Pacific* and *Great Northern Railways* built lines in. Early in September the first issue of the Phoenix *Pioneer* made its appearance, and with the exception of Rossland, the output of the mines far exceeded the combined production of all other mining camps in the province.

An article in the 1958 *Annual Report* of the Boundary Historical Society relates that "by the spring of 1900 the ladies of Phoenix were delicately holding up their skirts as they crossed from boardwalk to boardwalk on dusty Old Ironsides Avenue. Phoenix Stage Lines, MacIntyre & MacDonald, proprietors, made two daily round trips from Greenwood to Phoenix and visitors to Phoenix might choose from a variety of available hotel accommodation. "Finest Wines, Liquors and Cigars" were offered at the Brooklyn (Phoenix's first class hotel), at the Bellevue, the Mint, the Union, the Imperial (table board seven dollars a week), at the Norden, the Maple Leaf, the Butte, the Cottage, Black's, the Golden, King's, Queen's and Victoria House."

"The cuisine of the Brooklyn Hotel was famous and splendid banquets

Train wrecks were a frequent sight near old Phoenix.

took place there on special occasions. The menu of the Christmas Day dinner of 1911, for example, offers among a variety of other delicacies such gourmets' fare as Russian Caviar on Toast, Blue Point Oysters on the Half Shell, Green Turtle Soup, Broiled Salmon Trout with Anchovy Butter, Young Turkey and Chestnut Stuffing, Domestic Duck with Apple Stuffing, English Plum Pudding with Brandy Sauce, plus an assortment of wines, punches and cocktails."

The social life, the *Report* noted, had to do with the four churches and the Miners Hall in which were located a theatre, banquet hall and the finest ballroom in the interior of the province.

The city had a hospital, a four-room school, which like the others at the time served up education like a dose of castor oil, a skating rink, a brewery, stores, banks, undertakers and dressmakers and the "highest judge in Canada."

In his own lifetime, W. R. "Judge Willie" Williams became a legend. Standing well over six feet in height, he administered the law in the highest incorporated city in Canada, and like the famous Judge Begbie of the Cariboo, many tales have been told about him.

Phoenix was noted for its "big games" and although Judge Willie was on the bench, he sometimes found it difficult to keep to the straight and narrow, especially if, in all innocence his feet led him to where his mind told him he shouldn't go. On one occasion, he got taken to the cleaners in a "fixed" game, which ended when he had his gaming friends thrown into jail. Next morning they appeared in court before him.

"Now, gentlemen," he said, "it's my turn."

Magistrate Williams was in Phoenix from 1897 to 1913 and in later stories to the Grand Forks *Gazette* he admitted that life in the city was free and easy, but "the spirit of the hive was such that no one could be in want or suffering, that the whole community would rise up as a unit and help them on to a better life. The milk of human kindness was in everybody's heart, the hand of friendship was always extended to the downtrodden, the sign of welcome was on the door mat and the latch string always hung on the outside of the door where anyone could pull it and walk in and help themselves."

With the end of the war in 1918 the price of copper dropped. The Granby company continued to operate until the summer of 1919 when a strike in the coal fields of the Crows Nest Pass forced a closure of the smelters at Greenwood and Grand Forks.

Stairs leading to nothing.

Phoenix, 1961.

When, in the fall of 1919 the Fernie strike was over, the price of copper had dropped still further, Phoenix, which had no other industry but the mines, began to die. Soon all the houses were empty, and the windows boarded up. By 1920 wrecking crews arrived on the scene, and the stores, the churches, hospital and the skating rink were dismantled to be re-erected in other areas.

When the exodus was complete, only one man remained. He was a one-armed Belgian known as "4-Paw", who moved all of his possessions into the City Hall and took up residence there as mayor, chief of police and magistrate.

It was not long before he found a Doukhobor removing some property, whereupon he decked himself with revolver, handcuffs and police badge and proceeded to arrest the suspect and put him in the lock-up. The prisoner, however, escaped and "4-Paw" was a bitter man at such discourtesy.

"4-Paw" has gone, and so has Phoenix. It wasn't even allowed to mellow into old age.

179

General view of Fairview in the mid-1890's.

Anaconda, Boundary Falls, Fairview, Olalla, Keremeos Centre and East Princeton

To be a successful ghost town doesn't require any stature or fame, although it is true some previous publicity will be of help in keeping the memories alive.

Success is really measured by what the people who lived there thought, what they did and what they hoped for. The little things which gave them pleasure, like going for a walk in the forest or along a river bank on a Sunday afternoon, or just plain a-sitting on the porch with the hot sun pressing on their back and letting the world go by. Perhaps this place of shuttered windows, fallen down homes, or even bare foundations sticking up through the weeds had been a wonderful place to grow up in. Now it lies shattered. But to those who lived there, the good memories haven't gone that way. And, as for the bad, well, that's in the past; forget them, and remember only the good things.

In this manner success has come quietly to some of the ghost towns on the next leg of our journey—Anaconda, for instance. It was a suburb of Greenwood, and like that city, it looked up to the domineering, ugly brick stack which once belched sulphurous smoke as the smelting fires below extracted copper from the ores shipped down from nearby mines. It had little life of its own; it owed all to the B.C. Copper Company smelter, and to big, brassy Greenwood, and this must have been rather galling. For Greenwood was a johnny-come-lately, appearing on the scene a full three years after C. A. R. Lambly laid out his townsite in 1892. Perhaps the only thing Anaconda could claim sole possession of was a post office, opened by James McNichol on November 1, 1896, but Greenwood had beaten them to this mark by eleven months.

It must be admitted that Lambly's townsite remained dormant for several years, but when it did get going, Anaconda received an accolade from the press on the coast.

"Hardly three months ago [Anaconda] was in a wilderness of stunted pine trees," said *The Province* on August 8, 1896. "Today it has two general stores, restaurants, two hotels (Snodgrass & Kelly's Palace and the Anaconda owned by a man named Nicholas), one really first class assay office, etc. etc. The streets, too, are broad and well graded," and the town, along with Greenwood, the report continued, showed a "display of confidence in the future of the country which does them infinite credit."

Another compliment came in the 1902 *Report of the B.C. Minister of Mines*. Anaconda, it said, is "making steady progress, being in favour as a place of residence."

It had a little newspaper which reported the usual tidbits of local gossip, the coming and goings, the whist parties, the lost dogs and the bargains. Its pages never had earth-shaking stories, and those items which did appear were probably old news by the time the paper hit the streets, for babbling tongues are faster at that job than the fastest flat bed press.

If you were to take a man-in-the-street poll in Greenwood today, few would have ever heard of Anaconda, and fewer still could point the way to its "broad and well graded streets," and its "etc. etc." Yet once Anaconda lived, quietly and serenely, and although it is gone, surely there will be someone yet who will stand up and say, "It was a wonderful place to grow up in."

To the west of Anaconda stood the baby of the Boundary country's smelter towns, Boundary Falls. This plant, often called the Sunset Smelter, was owned by the Montreal & Boston Copper Company and was "blown in" in 1902; but with the drastic drop in copper prices

The Fairview Hotel, the "Big Teepee" and one of the finest hostelries in the Interior, about 1900.

Olalla, a sleepy little ghost town beside the main highway between Keremeos and Penticton, was destroyed by fire in spring of 1963.

following the First World War operations ceased. The closing of the smelter put Boundary Falls in the same position as Phoenix, and with nothing else to cling to but the mines, it soon vanished.

All that remain of this smelter town are the ruins of the smelter and a great pile of black slag, the refuse from the plant. Gone, too, is the mammoth chimney, the status symbol of the smelter town. After prowling around these ruins seeking to reconstruct in our mind the days when the Sunset was going full blast—and finding it very difficult to do—we headed for the Okanagan Valley and the village of Oliver.

High above the lush fruit ranches, up a steep narrow twisting road, once stood Fairview, a loosely knit mining community which boasted, aside from its mineral production, the largest hotel in the interior, the Fairview, often called the Big Teepee.

As a town, Fairview's life was short. It was laid out in 1897, but five years later a fire ravaged the community. It was the beginning of the end.

With the development of a Soldier Settlement scheme at Oliver following the First World War, some of the remaining buildings were moved down to the new townsite. The last building on the old site, the jail, was torn down in 1962. Now cactus and sage brush cover the town. Only the cemetery and the ruins of the mine workings remain.

Gold was discovered here in 1887 by Fred Gwatkins and George Sheenan, who turned their interests in what became the Stemwinder mine over to an English and American syndicate in the early '90s. By 1893 a Mr. Kline had opened the Golden Gate Hotel which soon earned—no doubt justifiably—the nickname Bucket of Blood. Shortly afterwards came the Miners Rest, the Fairview, and the Blue House, not forgetting Moffatt's all-important saloon.

It was lamented by some that Fairview never pushed itself forward, that if some initiative had been shown, it could have been as good a place as any below the border. It was only an excuse, for in the battle for existence a mining town is only as good as the mines, and even if the finest town in the world had been laid out at Fairview, it would have been, in the end, only a bigger ghost town.

Another of the small ghost towns is Olalla, set back a few yards from the Southern Trans-Provincial Highway just north of Keremeos. It was another mining town of one long street lined on either side with homes, stores, a school, and probably a saloon or two.

The fortress-like ruins of the cement plant at East Princeton.

Olalla in the early days received little attention from the press, except when a mild scandal arose. It is said that a friend of John Oliver was involved in the Olalla Mining Company, which claimed to be capitalized for eight million dollars and had rich holdings. As a member of the B.C. Legislature, and later a premier of the province, Honest John was, so the mining man thought, in a good position to do a few favours, as for instance, building a road to the mine at government expense.

Oliver agreed to mention the company to the government, but no more than that. When it was learned that the company was not as genuine as it first appeared, that the government had rallied to give some support to the company, and that Oliver's name was mixed up in it, the honourable member for Delta was furious. John Oliver could talk, and talk he did, but when he arose, opposition benchers would whisper "oo-la-lah!". And John, under his shaggy beard had to grin and bear it.

The ghost of Olalla lasted until the late spring of 1963. Then, the scourge of the wooden mining camps—fire—swept through the town, devouring it.

Between Olalla and Keremeos stand a forlorn hotel and several decrepit buildings on the opposite side of the highway, the relics of Keremeos Centre, once a stopping place on the old road to the mines of Hedley and Nickle Plate. The hotel, the Central, was operated by Halliburton Tweddle, and in the Keremeos *Trumpet* for July 10, 1908 we find that the Central Hotel gave "Special attention to Commercial men,

Tourists and Landseekers. Headquarters for all Stage Routes. Livery Stable in connection. Good Table. Large airy and comfortable rooms. Free bus to and from all trains."

It has been empty for years, and the bar now reposes in a commercial "wild west" ghost town with the improbable sign that gashes in the mahogany were caused by drunken gun slingers.

The Central Hotel was still in operation when Princeton, on the banks of the Similkameen River, was calling itself the "Payroll City." Perhaps a couple of gentlemen named John George and John Budd dropped in for a glass of champagne or a finger or two of whisky to tell of their grandiose plans for the area to the westward.

These two formed a company known as the B.C. Portland Cement Company, sold shares locally, and obtained a hundred acres of land from the old Allison Estate on One Mile Creek on which to build a factory and a modern city with wide boulevards, fine homes, big business blocks and schools. And so began East Princeton.

Purchasers paid from $200 to $700 a lot, and, said the *Similkameen Star* of Princeton on August 9, 1911, "Those erecting buildings within a specified time receive discounts on their lots."

In the first four weeks sales totalled $20,000 and the *Star* noted "the lots bring a higher price than improved lots in much older towns. This is due entirely to the fact that the owner is making it a model town from the start and giving good values with the property."

While this land-booming was going on from an office in the Pacific Building in Vancouver, fortress-like buildings were being erected for the cement plant, and a half-million dollars was literally poured into its construction. The *Great Northern Railway* spent $60,000 on a spur line, and early in 1913 the massive machinery began to turn.

Utilizing a nearby limestone and gypsum deposit, the plant produced a high grade of cement, and then, suddenly the wheels stopped. Nine months had passed since the gala opening and now they were never to roll again.

What happened? Nobody knows. In fact, it has been suggested that the people of Princeton were too heart sick to investigate the cause. Today, stalwart walls and crumbled masonry provide shade for grazing cattle, and probably, in a few strong boxes in Princeton there are still some gilt-edged certificates of the B.C. Portland Cement Company.

It is best to forget them.

Early view of Granite Creek, once the third largest community in British Columbia.

Granite Creek

LET US now consider the game of Chance. John, it seems, neither toiled any more than he had to, nor did he spin, and yet, on the banks of Granite Creek, near Princeton, where he loafed one hot day in July 1885, a cairn has been erected to his memory.

This marker to John Chance stands besides the bleak, weather-beaten shell of the town which grew up around his discovery claim. At one time Granite Creek, or Granite City, was the third largest community in British Columbia, following Victoria and New Westminster. At the height of its glory, Granite Creek had 13 hotels and "temples of Bacchus", nine grocery stores, two jewellers, two blacksmiths, a shoemaker, a drug store and about 56 cabins strung along two muddy streets called Miners and Government.

It was a wild, swinging town, where everybody carried a revolver stuck in his belt, and to the miners from the Cariboo and the Kootenay who drifted into town during the rush it was hardly believable. One of these was Sam Evans, who, in the *Colonist* for October 14, 1885 says "some of the miners affect revolvers which they openly carry upon their persons, the principal portion of the class being formed of ranchers, cowboys and halfbreeds who gallop all over and if gold is on the surface they find it, but they would not sink three feet for anything."

Of this type, John Chance was typical.

For details of the "game of Chance" we have Mrs. John Fall Allison, pioneer Similkameen Valley settler, to thank for setting down her reminiscences which appeared in the Vancouver *Province* on May 17, 1931.

"The cowboys," she wrote, "during slack time, drew their wages and dressing themselves in the most elaborate cowpuncher style, rode down the valley. They were Bill McKeon, Billy Elwell and Harry Hobb, three of the best and most cheerful perverters of the truth I ever knew. What they did or told at Oroville [Washington] I don't know, but they returned in a week smiling and said it would not be dull long, and next day, sure enough, several strange men passed with pack horses loaded with miners' equipment; some even stopped to ask about the 'new strike.'

"There was one party of eight or ten men with Wild Goose Bill Jenkins at their head that insisted that there had been a very big strike. He had seen the gold dust the cowboys brought down to Oroville with them. I told them to ask the boys; they did, but did not get much satisfaction. Finally, they struck it rich and named their claim 'Rich Bar'; such it proved to be.

"They worked hard, except one man, Johnny Chance, who was too lazy to work, so they made him cook, but as the weather grew hotter that was too much exertion for him, so his partners gave him a gun and told him to get a few grouse. He departed and strolled about until he found a nice cool creek that emptied itself into the river. Here he threw himself down till sunset, his feet paddling the cold water, when a ray of light fell on something yellow; he drew it towards him, picked it up. It was a nugget of pure gold! He looked into the water again, there was another, and another. He pulled out his buckskin purse and slowly filled it. Then, picking up his gun, strolled back to camp where he became a hero and the discoverer of Granite Creek."

The date was July 5, 1885.

Twenty days later, readers of the *Colonist*, if their eyes happened to catch a little item at the bottom of the second column of page 3 for July 25, 1885, might have seen this laconic headline: "Another Gold Strike". The story told how 20 claims had been staked and the men were making from $8 to $10 per day.

At first the diggings were at the mouth of the creek, but the miners, restless as only miners can be, moved slowly upstream, confident that better prospects could be found. Through water up to their waists the prospectors, some of whom had been cowboys only the day before, splashed their way up the canyon, so that, by September two and a half miles of the creek had been staked. There was, even at that early date, hardly enough room to move about and pile tailings. There were, at this time, 500 white men and an equal number of Chinese working the stream.

By the end of July, it was reported two men had rocked out $400 in one day, and on September 17 the *Colonist* said, "The claim of Mr. Chance is paying from fifty to seventy-five dollars per day to the man, while others are paying as well."

The stampede was on, and by the end of October, J. F. Allison reported "a town rapidly springing up" with substantial hotels replacing temporary tent ones, and there was talk of sending samples to the London and Colonial Exhibition the following year.

Men who had been employed on construction of the *Canadian Pacific Railway*, now nearing completion, flocked to the new camp, and others came south from Barkerville and west from the Kootenay.

"Stories told of their success," said the *Colonist* on September 18, "are so exciting that Mr. Richter hesitates to repeat them here."

Remarks like that did nothing to stop the wild rush, just as it does nothing to help the historian, and as winter set in and many of the miners "came out," Sam Pearse, a '58er from the days of the Fraser River rush, sagely told the press that Granite Creek was "the best poor man diggings he ever saw."

"It is no uncommon sight," said the *Colonist* on January 3, "to get up in the morning and find the town almost deserted, running off on the craze of some new discovery."

And then, with the smell of spring in the air, the young man's fancy was turned to Granite Creek and a new wave of miners hit the stream. "Ho for Granite Creek!" advertised the B.C. Express Company, and

John Chance, discoverer of gold on Granite Creek in 1885.

Robert Stevenson, who had been Cariboo Cameron's partner on Williams Creek, got together his pack train to haul in supplies from Hope. Granite Creek hotel owners, at the Driard, the Stanley, Cariboo House, Adelphi and the Miners Rest, to name a few, checked over their stocks of whisky and cigars, for these and not the beds were their stock in trade.

To one of these hotels, Andy Gordon "the strongest man on the creek" packed in a 400-pound stove from Hope on his back, and to celebrate the arrival, the owner threw the bar open for free drinks. But big Andy Gordon wanted to drink alone, so he threw everybody else out, shut the door, and sat down in front of the newly arrived stove to enjoy the free hospitality.

The reports which reached the outside were grossly exaggerated, for,

Ruins of the F. P. Cook store at Granite Creek.

to those who arrived late, Granite Creek was no El Dorado. Professor Menzies, who, the *Colonist* said "has returned to the practice of his magnetic powers to this city [Victoria]" spent five weeks in the Similkameen, and on July 11, 1886 warned that "at Granite Creek there are many good honest, hard working men who cannot get employment and under necessity are even compelled to seek the garbage from the hotels." Summing up, the writer of the *Colonist* item said the moral of the story was "don't go to Granite Creek."

Very early in the rush the Chinese, most of whom had been working for Andrew Onderdonk on *CPR* construction, descended on the camp and in short order began to buy up all available claims. In October 1885 one of them found a smooth, worn nugget worth $83 and a couple of months later, another found one worth $900. But these were not typical of the nuggets found in Granite Creek, and the remark of one of the Celestials to the gold commissioner may be closer to the mark.

When asked how much gold he had taken out, the Chinese replied, "Not enough!"—and this became his unofficial name.

However, if there was "not enough" gold in the Creek to satisfy the desires of the Chinese, then there was another way of making a profit. In 1859 a Canadian named Adam Beam had found gold on Rock Creek, a hundred miles to the east, and until the great opening up of the Cariboo gold fields in 1861 and 1862 it proved to be a camp of major importance. Gradually, interest in Rock Creek diminished and it was left to the Chinese to work. Rock Creek gold, however, was not worth nearly as much as the gold found on Granite, so the Chinese at Rock Creek used to send their gold over to their countrymen at Granite to sell. The racket worked well for a short time until the merchants and gold buyers awoke to the fact that the Celestials were taking them to the cleaners.

With the Chinese holding most of the claims, and the cowboys firmly believing that work was the curse of the drinking man, the saloon keepers were the ones who made the most money. And to keep in business they had to be pretty fast with both their feet and their fists.

On September 19, 1885 the *Colonist* reported there had been a murder at Granite Creek. It seemed that a James Nolan was bargaining with a cowboy over the sale of a claim, and during the negotiations the cowboy drew a revolver and shot Nolan through the head. With two companions the cowboy fled to the border, hotly chased by four armed men bent on collecting a $1000 reward put up by the miners.

Ten days later the *Colonist* printed a follow up to the original story and headlined it simply "Correct Version." The man's name was not Nolan, but Newland; he was not murdered, and there was no claim for sale. The desperado was "an amateur cowboy partly intoxicated riding through the camp and firing at every object.

"Newland made some deprecatory remarks and the cowboy, who is a dead-shot, attempted to put a hole through his hat" but unfortunately grazed his forehead and Newland dropped. The miners offered a reward of $150 to the man who could bring him in, and a typical cowboy, a little fellow, started with his Winchester and returned with his prisoner. Newland rode right out of camp and up to Savona where he "is now all right again and states the shooting was accidental."

"The cowboy who brought in the man was sworn in as a special constable and took the prisoner to Allisons', though threatened by the gang with rough handling if he did so. However he defied them all and conducted the man safely to his destination."

From there the gun-happy cowboy, whose name was given only as Shorty, was taken down to New Westminster to stand trial but, as the *Colonist* put it, "he had the sympathy of the whole camp. Mrs. Allison is raising money to defend him, a large number of the miners subscribing who would be glad to see him out of the scrape, as he is a harmless fellow and had no intent to hit Newland."

In September 1886 the *Colonist* said "a good many storekeepers have failed or left" and added there are still "so many saloons that all are not able to make a legitimate living."

The truth of Granite Creek was now beginning to be grasped, and it was summed up by Mr. Allison in a report to the *Colonist* on October 22. "Mr. Allison said gold is being taken out of Granite Creek and says it will keep a few men employed every year, but there was never anything to warrant last year's boom."

Most of the miners drifted away. The hotels, with the exception of the Cariboo House and the Granite Creek Hotel, closed down. All the merchants, except F. P. Cook, left but Granite Creek did not die rapidly.

Mr. Sam Adler, one of the pioneers of Quesnelle Forks and the Cariboo described Granite in November as "the worst mining camp he has known since 1850."

"Those who are remaining are only holding out in the hope of an improvement. If gold is secured in paying quantities it will be found in the hill claims. Some of these latter have paid wages. A house that cost $600 in labour alone was sold for two glasses of whisky. Another that cost $1500 was sold for $15 and cut into firewood. Goods are being sacrificed. About forty white men still remain."

On April 4, 1907 the town burned. The fire started in Cook's combined store and dwelling place, which stood on the site of the present Chance cairn, and quickly spread. The only buildings which survived were "Judge" Thomas Murphy's quarters, the deserted Cariboo House and the jail, which legend says was useless from the very beginnings as its windows lacked bars. The *Similkameen Star* once described the Judge as being "in Granite so long that he remembers when Mr. Columbus sailed up the Tulameen to discover America."

The Cariboo House was re-opened as a "temple of Bacchus", but in time, it burned down. F. P. Cook re-established his store and continued to operate it until 1912 when the business was moved to Coalmont a mile away.

Dredges were brought in, and the whole course of Granite Creek was altered, so that the original creek has dried up and is as forlorn as the remains of the town standing bleakly on the benchland above. And here, the frail, hollow shell of Cook's general store, young in age, as far as Granite Creek is concerned, stands mutely as one of the pawns in the "game of Chance."

The Japanese internment camp at Tashme on the Hope-Princeton Highway.

Tashme

IN 1942 the old Dewdney Trail out from Hope witnessed a tragic procession, the arrival at the Trites Ranch, or 14-Mile, of thousands of up-rooted Japanese and Japanese-Canadians who were removed from the coastal regions after the attack on Pearl Harbour.

From Steveston at the mouth of the Fraser, from the densely populated "Little Tokyo" of Vancouver's east end, they were herded to Hastings Park, and from there many were sent to temporary road camps at such remote pinpoints on the map as Tete Jaune Cache, Thunder River, Albreda, Red Pass Junction and Lucerne. Within months permanent homes had been found for them in the ghost towns of Sandon, Minto City, and in Kaslo, Greenwood, New Denver and Lillooet. Others were moved to the prairies and to eastern Canada, in one of the greatest forced migrations in Canada's history, second only to the expulsion of the Acadians from Nova Scotia.

As well as revitalizing some dead and dying towns in B.C.'s interior, a new town was born in the heart of the mountains west of Hope, known as Tashme. Sounding Japanese, the name Tashme actually comes from the names of officers of the B.C. Security Commission, which consisted of Austin C. Taylor, Vancouver businessman, John Shirras, of the B.C Provincial Police and F. J. Mead of the Royal Canadian Mounted Police.

Here a total of 347 homes of rough lumber construction were built, sealed on the outside with tar-paper, and with building paper on the inside. An "apartment block", hospital, general store and a sawmill with a capacity of 6500 feet per day were built. A 25 k.w. electric plant was installed to serve the principle buildings, but in the main, this 20th-century war-time village was lit by primitive coal-oil lamps. Six water-mains were put in with a tap serving three or four houses, and a bath house for every 50 cabins.

Despite these inconveniences, life at Tashme was far from being unbearable, the major blight being the fact the residents could not leave.

"But," said the Japanese weekly, the *New Canadian*, "though people live and work together, their thoughts are by no means similar. Some are still bitter and hurt and care not whether the community progresses or not. And out of this bitterness of their feelings, they wish to strike out blindly in return for what they feel the injustice done to them, grows discord and disharmony. On the other hand are those others 'taking life as it comes.' They left their self pity behind them when they moved and cheerfully tackle the issues before them, for they know the real answer to the question: 'where will grumbling, dissatisfaction, spitefulness and self pity get anyone in this evacuation centre?

"Probably the older generation here find life most satisfactory, for their days of fun and frolic are over and to them a secluded quiet round is sufficient . . . "

One of those who found life at Tashme pleasant was a Mr. F. Taguchi, formerly of the Fraser Valley, who wrote:

"Generally speaking facilities at Tashme are very good. We are living in one room on the second storey of one of the so-called apartment blocks. Running water, both hot and cold, is a great blessing, especially since we are able to bathe every night.

"There is one general store here and a butcher shop and though no luxuries are provided, still no great inconvenience is met.

"However, often the customers must stand in long lines waiting to be served and this is hard upon mothers with babies or small children who find the waiting very tiresome. But coming from the country, we do admit to a feeling of thankfulness on the whole that conditions are as good as we have found them."

Affairs in this community were at first in the hands of the "construction committee" but by popular vote on December 7, 1942 a new committee of 50 members was established to administer the civic affairs of the 2600 persons living in the camp. In addition there was the Tashme Youth Organization, enlisting members between the ages of 16 and 35 and the Young Buddhist Association with 80 members, and a troop of Boy Scouts. On the 24th of May gala celebrations were held, complete with the crowning of a May Queen, and the local school published a 16-page mimeographed paper called *Tales from Tashme*.

But boredom, the awareness that it was impossible to go beyond well-defined borders, and the memory of life in the big city and the Saturday night parties in Steveston were difficult to overcome, even though everything possible was done to make life for the internees as pleasant as possible under the circumstances.

"It may sound rather contradictory," wrote "W. K." in the *New Canadian*, "but a description of the conditions under which we are living in this wartime settlement might be summed up simply in our own boredom. With so little physical discomfort, it seems that we have but few problems to grapple with and few worries to occupy our minds. So that seeing the same row of houses, the same faces all around, the same children at play on the green and spacious grounds surrounding the village, we often think how wonderful it would be to visit Vancouver once again. And yet, here the air is cleaner. The water—for bacteria and chlorine—is cold and clear, and we have no politicians to wrangle with the scientists over it. Firewood is delivered to each house on trucks and garbage is taken away once every week. A high point in the day's routine is the visit of the lamp-lighter, who cleans the lamp, and adds a ration of coal oil. We have yet to catch him serenading or sprinkling anything but soot . . . All of us, in short, are congratulating ourselves on how good conditions actually are. But with human perverseness, we tire of looking at the peaceful rows of houses every day, twenty-two in the first row and thirteen in the last—and yearn for the hustle and bustle of the big city."

The able-bodied men worked on construction of the Hope-Princeton Highway, or in the camp, and besides the main camp at Tashme a secondary one was established at Mile 12, housing the road workers. A soya plant was put into operation and the sawmill kept others busy.

The camp was opened in September 1942 and closed on August 12, 1946, and soon thereafter, the wreckers moved in to rip the town apart and return the Trites Ranch to its agricultural existence.

None of the encampment buildings remain, but the ruins of the camp at Mile 12 can still be seen and you can wander amongst the frame houses, peeping into open doors and walk across rotted wooden floors. And through the glassless windows, peer out and see the remnants of what was a valiant, short lived effort to maintain a garden.

In the summer of the year, flowers still bloom among the rocks, unsown and ungathered.

Steamboat Mountain

ON A HOT day in June, 1911, J. H. Gerrie, a former editorial staffer with the New York *Herald*, sat down before his typewriter in the editorial offices of the Hope *News & Gold Trail* in "the Spokane of British Columbia" and began punching out one of the gushiest pieces of prose ever inflicted on the reading public.

"I have just come out of El Dorado over the trail of the gods," he wrote, and in breathless excitement he used up just about every cliche in the book many times over, and continued it for several columns spread over two issues.

If you happen to be of the generation which remembers those barnstorming days of 1910-1912, the name Steamboat Mountain will bring to mind many memories. If it was as an investor, then we're sorry to bring the subject up.

Mr. Gerrie's "trail of the gods" was roughly speaking the present-day Hope-Princeton Highway, that is, as far as Mile 120, which in the days of the rush was called 23-Mile, being that distance from Hope. From 23-Mile, the trail turned south to follow the Skagit River to a point just a few miles above the international boundary.

Today a simpler route exists, up the Silver Creek road, from the Trans-Canada Highway just below Hope, and at the head of the 40-mile drive lies our goal—a pile of bleached lumber. The ghost-town hunter, however, may not be disappointed, for the drive in is a beauty.

It was on the Skagit River, in 1879, that W. L. Flood and James Corrigan, according to tradition, built a raft to float down the river to a gold showing on Ruby Creek, a tributary of the Skagit. They named their raft *Steamboat* and the point from which they pushed off came to be called Steamboat Landing. In the course of time the mountain immediately behind was named Steamboat Mountain. Unfortunately this colourful name is no more, for modern maps call it Shawatum.

During the 1880s there was considerable interest in the Skagit area as a mining country, but no prospects were forthcoming to cause any real excitement. However, in July 1910, two prospectors, Dan Greenwald and W. A. Stevens, entered the country following a tip from an old-timer in Humboldt County, Nevada.

"Several times," the *News & Gold Trail* reported on February 24, 1911, "the two gold seekers thought they had come to the right stream, as they had secured good pannings from several of the small creeks, but none of these exactly answered the description given to Greenwald.

"It was not until the 15th of June, though the prospectors had been in the neighbourhood for nearly a month, that they finally discovered Steamboat Creek. When they came upon the stream they found gold in its bed and knew it was the stream for which they had been hunting. They made their camp at the foot of the mountain and began to prospect the ledges on either side of the creek simultaneously.

"They were in no hurry because summer was just beginning; and in the valley were plenty of deer and fish in the Skagit River."

Word soon "leaked out" and a rush to the Skagit began. In October 1910, Vancouver promoter C. D. Rand announced he had acquired "a large interest" in the discovery claims and added that development work would be carried on during the winter, and a large stamp mill was planned for the following summer.

People from all walks of life flocked to Steamboat. And we must not forget the poets—heavens no, for without a poet what good is a gold rush!

This great epic poem was "composed and sung by Harvey P. Leonard for Christmas 1910."

STEAMBOAT

There's a place called Hope in the country
Not many miles from Beaver Lake
Where the boys in the spring will be rushing
Their chances with fortune to take.
I know when the Lord made old Eden
He thought He did the job fine;
But Adam found pay dirt was missing
While Steamboat has many a mine.

CHORUS

Take me down, down
Where the Steamboat trail goes—
There we'll bury our sorrows
Our cares and our woes.
Get a claim while you can
And the diggings are new,
If you linger long, all you'll get is a view,
Instead of the rain we've the real "Mountain Dew"
Down where the Steamboat Trail goes.

Just think of Hope when it's famous,
When skyscrapers loom up in view,
The trolley line completed,
The G.N.R. to Hope running too!
A statue to Greenwald erected,
Will stand in the City Hall Square—
The days will be always so sunny,
Of old age they only die there.

When the years have gone and the founders
Of Hope have long turned to clay—
Your heirs on the tombstone might wonder
At lines which to others would say:
There "lies" Vinson, the man of the stories,
Stevens and Parnaby, too—
While Walter Grey is toasting in Hades,
A place where the heat suits a few.

As far as Steamboat was concerned, the hucksters had a field day, what with promoting mining stock and townsites, but here the picture gets a little confusing, and in some cases we can't be sure that the promoters knew what was going on. Not one, not two, but three townsites sprang up, and their names were Steamboat, Steamboat Mountain and Steamboat City. Ever helpful, the *News & Gold Trail* ventured that "as the names are confusing we will designate them by their hotels."

Therefore, Steamboat was known as McIntyre & Raymonds Hotel, and was made famous, or at least the promoters would have us so believe, as being the "Steamboat with the Buildings in!" By May 1911, land agents J. C. Thorn & Company of Vancouver announced "several brick buildings ready. Other buildings under construction."

Steamboat Mountain townsite was owned by "Alaska Jack" Given, and boasted a two-storey hotel owned by Messrs Still & McDonald, a store, a tonsorial emporium and six cabins.

Steamboat City, a little farther away, but still snugly close to the others, was owned by Alfred Jarvis and was surveyed into 90 lots. Jarvis owned a hotel and there was also a store. On the drawing boards were aerial tramways to the mines, etc.

Of all, Steamboat was the most ambitious, and coast daily newspapers carried full page advertisements expounding the future of the community in glowing terms.

On June 15 it was announced that a board of trade had been formed at a meeting in McIntyre & Raymond's Hotel, with David Sloan as president.

"It will act in place of town council, taking care of sanitation, fire protection, street paving and lighting," said the *News*.

With the opening of the season of 1911, the excitement reached the point of hysteria. The two newspapers in Hope, the *News* and the *Steamboat Nugget*, which later merged into the *West Yale Review*, were frequently quoted by the metropolitan dailies and there was no doubt in anybody's mind that the Steamboat camp was going places. The trail to the mines "was like a path in Stanley Park" quoth the *News*.

On June 1 the *News* headlined, "Is Steamboat richer than Porcupine?" and the writer of the story suggested that, yea verily, it was so. In his mind, Steamboat was indeed richer than Porcupine.

In the early days of the rush whenever Greenwald or Stevens came to Hope the whole town turned out to cheer and both would humbly accept the adoration of the crowd like Oriental potentates, and would generously bestow to the faithful a well-remembered hand-clasp or a wave of the hand. But early in 1911 it was noticed that Messrs. Greenwald and Stevens had absented themselves from Hope for a considerable period. To Mr. C. D. Rand in his Vancouver office, and to his fellow directors in the Steamboat Mountain Gold Mines Ltd., it was a matter of grave concern, for all hell was about to break loose.

The public, however, kept pouring money into Steamboat, blissfully ignorant of what was really going on—until June. Then, Mr. Rand admitted they were indeed in grave trouble. He had learned the mine had been salted!

"So skillfully was it done," said the *West Yale Review* in September, "that for a time nobody suspected it. There was a little gold to be found in the bed of the creek and an 8-inch vein of low values found on the mountain, both circumstances lending support to the story of the rich deposit outcropping at the summit."

It is said the mine was salted with shavings from U.S. gold coins, minted in Denver, which were cemented into surface cracks and upon fragments of rock.

Apparently the first suspicion that something was wrong occurred in the fall of 1910. If that were the case, the logical question to be asked is: Why wasn't something done about it right away? The answer was given by W. F. Bradley, foreman of the mine, and one of the early arrivals in the camp.

"All kept silent," he said, "partly because publication of the truth would destroy the market value of other properties, and partly in honest expectation that genuine discoveries would be made."

Greenwald and Stevens, knowing the jig was up, had crossed the border, taking with them a good sized chunk of the treasury.

Dan went to South America, coming back to the States in September 1911, only a few months after the Steamboat bubble had burst, and to a reporter in New York he piously denounced the "wicked men who lure poor miners to worthless ground by sending out false reports."

Said the *West Yale Review*: "Dan's nerve food is a success."

Stevens, a few months later commited suicide. It was said he died from remorse — but not on account of Steamboat Mountain. One of his California projects had collapsed.

PART VI

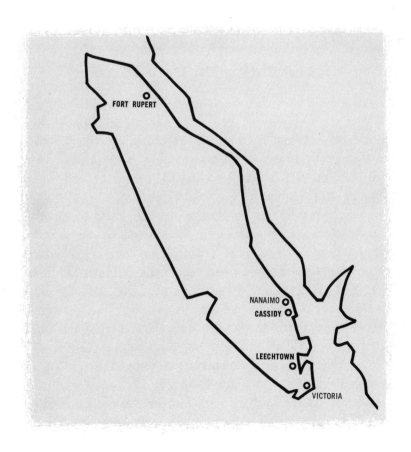

Kennedy Flat during the 1865 gold rush to Leech River.

Leechtown, Cassidy and Fort Rupert

IT TAKES time and money, and a lot of each, to visit all the ghost towns of Vancouver Island, and lacking both of these essentials, we had to content ourselves with staring wistfully at a map, fingering old newspaper clippings and waiting for our ship to come in.

But close to Victoria lies its Barkerville, the ghost town of Leechtown, sometimes called Leech River in the old records. So, armed with a notebook of jottings taken from the Victoria *Colonist* of the middle 1860s, we drove up the Island Highway, over the scenic Malahat Drive, towards Shawnigan Lake. Just before we reached the Lake, a sign pinned to a tree pointed south to Leechtown.

In the 1860s a more direct way was followed up from Sooke but time has erased the old trail, and unless you catch a CNR way-freight and get off in the middle of nowhere, this route, through the Greater Victoria watershed, is the only way.

It was on July 14, 1864 that a former member of the Royal Engineers, Peter Leech, discovered gold bearing gravels in the creek which now bears his name. Now it seemed to the residents of Victoria, who were jealous of the golden wealth of the mainland, here was their own Cariboo, right on their front doorstep, and they proceeded to make the most of it.

It has been said that Victoria was well-nigh deserted when the fever broke out, and a theatre notice of the time hoped that those who had not "concluded to visit Sooke" would patronize the performance of the seven young artists.

Transportation companies took out advertisements in the newspaper proclaiming "Ho! For Leech River!" A Mr. Charles Dechent, returning to Victoria from the gold field, told the *Colonist* on August 9 that "there is gold everywhere in more or less quantities. Even in the top dirt of both the benches which rise one above the other, prospects of from two to five cents have been found."

Reminiscent of the Barkerville camp was the Wake-Up Jake claim which was producing $22 a day, and a party of coloured miners was hard at work.

A month after the discovery a town of tents arose on Kennnedy Flat, named after Captain Arthur Edward Kennedy, the governor of Vancouver Island. Within six weeks, six general stores were in business, three hotels had opened their doors, and during the ensuing four months thirty temples of Bacchus were in full swing, giving the town a certain status.

"Kennedy Flat," noted the *Colonist* on April 28, 1865, "assumes the appearance of a thriving mining town, and were the streets but cleared of brush and stumps would make quite a picturesque scene. The townsite having been laid out and the streets marked, would it not be well to appropriate a couple of hundred dollars for this purpose?"

The best hotel in the camp was the Arrarat—"a most valuable acquisition to the mining community," the *Colonist* remarked on January 13, 1865— which contained a dozen rooms.

It was in this hotel that Governor Kennedy set up his headquarters for an inspection of the mines early in May 1865. On his arrival "a torch-light procession was formed and marched to the commissioner's tent to welcome His Excellency, singing on the way, 'For He's A Jolly Good Fellow'. Three cheers were given and acknowledged by His Excellency, when three more cheers were given."

The Arrarat, according to its advertisement in the *Colonist* for July 3, 1865 was "the only House fitted up for the accommodation of Ladies. The Proprietors [R. H. Johnson and R. L. Dixon] without regard to cost or trouble have put up a House that is the admiration of all lovers of cleanliness and good eating and which would not disgrace the great metropolis of Vancouver Island."

Within two or three years, Victoria's little Barkerville had ridden the crest of fame and died. Estimates indicate between $100,000 and $200,000 in gold was taken out, and single nuggets worth $70 were sometimes recovered. Most of the claims paid from $10 to $25 a day per man, and no great single bonanzas like the Williams Creek mines were found. By 1870 only a handful of miners remained, and these were mainly the patient Chinese busily cleaning up the old workings.

The road to Leechtown ended before a barrier, and an old gentleman, followed by a couple of youngsters, came out of a cabin to greet us. He was the watchman for the Sooke Lake Logging Company, and now the sole resident of Leechtown. From his front porch, it was less than a five minute walk to the cairn which commemorates the events that took place here a hundred years ago.

This marker, unveiled by the Honourable Randolph Bruce, lieutenant-governor of British Columbia, on September 15, 1928, was erected by the B.C. Historical Association from stones taken from the chimney of the gold commissioner's house.

Ponder for a minute on the man who used to warm himself beside this fireplace.

His name was Richard Golledge, former private secretary to the great James Douglas. It is claimed that he was the ghost writer for Douglas's few public utterances, and his connections in the early days of the colonies of Vancouver Island and British Columbia were unexcelled. As Gold Commissioner he was the most important man in the mining camp, for on his word and decision hung all the miners' law and their profits.

With Leechtown falling on hard times and decaying, Golledge followed the self-same path. He took to heavy drinking, and became within a few years a hopeless derelict. In 1884 he was convicted of stealing an Indian canoe and the *Colonist* said "it is hoped Golledge will rid the province of his presence, which has become distasteful to respectable people."

During the 1930s when depression blighted the province, a few unemployed men gathered on the banks of the Leech to wrest a living from the once-generous land. In the Second World War, Leechtown became a thriving community of 250 persons, but not as a mining camp. The forest wealth of the area was far greater than the mineral, but it, too, was transient. On the night of July 22-23, 1953 the Sooke Lumber

Company mill was burned, and Leechtown's life once again came to a close.

Perhaps the great trees which still stand in the townsite witnessed the gold fever of the 1860s and saw what no man today has seen or can imagine. Within a few years the half dozen or so flimsily-constructed buildings will have disappeared, and only the logging road, the idyllic river called the Leech, the monument, and, if the woodsmen spare them, those stately trees will remain.

But the old man back at the gates had hopes for Leechtown. Four claims were being worked in the vicinity, and he himself had picked up pieces of gold worth nearly two dollars each.

"It doesn't take many of those to make an ounce," he said, and pointing to one of the youngsters, his grandson, "he's a real little prospector."

"Yes," he said, "there's still gold here at Leechtown" and youth was there learning the ancient art of prospecting. Maybe this lad will find a ledge of gold the miners of old missed.

Between Nanaimo and Ladysmith once stood a model town, Cassidy, laid out and developed by the Granby Consolidated Mining, Smelting & Power Company Limited in 1919. It was a coal mining town and came into existence as a result of labour disturbances in the Crows Nest Pass which sometimes curtailed the flow of coal to the smelters in the Boundary district. The mine went into production in 1919 and the deposit was worked until 1932, the output going to the Granby smelter at Anyox on the northern B.C. coast and to the United States.

"The townsite," a company report states, "a more than ample area of level ground between hills, was planned to present a pleasing appearance. The streets were boulevarded and the homes were surrounded by lawns. The company had bought the entire stock of a nursery then on the market and there was an abundance of flowering shrubs and trees. The homes were modern and connected with adequate waterworks and sewerage systems. One of the finest athletic parks in the country was provided. Soccer football is a great game on the Island and the field was in frequent use. The hillside provided a natural grandstand.

"The rooming house was a two-storey building of unique construction and of pleasing architecture. It contained 80 rooms, each of which opened out on the veranda. They were steam heated, electric lighted, and provided with hot and cold water. The dining hall, change house, and first aid buildings were all high grade. The tipple and washery, powerhouse, carpenter, machine and blacksmith shops were thoroughly up to date. Pure water from the Nanaimo River was pumped to tanks on the nearby hill about a hundred feet above the townsite. A telephone system connected the surface plant and the underground workings."

Unfortunately, the Cassidy workings were plagued with gas, but luckily these pits never experienced the tragedies of the killer mine at Coal Creek. Another problem was the geological formation of the beds, with faults, pockets of coal and barren regions.

After the closing down of the workings the buildings were torn down and only the shell of the boarding house remains.

"The forest has regained its pre-eminence," concludes the Granby report. "If one visits the area in the spring, he will wonder at the sight of two parallel red lines through the green fir bush. Investigation will show that these are May trees in bloom. They once lined one of the streets."

Some time, perhaps, the odyssey to Vancouver Island will be resumed, but like Ulysses in the *Iliad* we had to be tied to the mast (the financial one) as the Sirens of the unvisited ghost towns on the wind-lashed West Coast and the northern part of the Island wailed their haunting call in our directions.

There was the voice from Fort Rupert, where a giant chimney and a few foundations testify to the existence of the first coal mining operations in British Columbia. Unlike other Hudson's Bay Company posts on the Pacific Coast, Fort Rupert's role was not as a trading post, but as a fortification to protect the coal miners from the depredations of the Indians.

Our friend Norman Hacking, marine editor of the *Province*, visited Fort Rupert in 1935 and described his odyssey to that historic ground in the *Province* for July 13, 1935.

"The sole residents of Fort Rupert today," he wrote, "are the Cadwallader family, who occupy the old fort property. Mr. Cadwallader's grandfather was Robert Hunt, a Hudson's Bay Company trader, who purchased the fort in 1878 when the Company withdrew. It has been owned by the family ever since, and a store is still operated on the site by Mr. and Mrs. Bill Cadwallader.

"Upon our arrival Mrs. Cadwallader showed us over the village and the remains of the old trading post. The bastion and the living quarters were torn down some years ago, but the original trading store remains. Its massive hand-hewn timbers, which were brought down from Fort Wrangell in 1849, are still in excellent shape.

"A huge stone fireplace stands in an open field, a reminder of days when all the meals were cooked over an open spit. Here and there are various sized cannonballs and other relics of fur trading days, while down on the beach lies an old cannon, half-buried in the sand, dated 1835."

The officers' quarters burned down in June 1889 and the *Colonist* in reporting this fire, has left us with a description of Fort Rupert as it originally stood.

"It [the officers' quarters] was 90 feet in length and 40 in width; built of rough hewn logs and pierced at regular intervals for the rifles, in case they were needed in the stormy days gone by.

"Around it ran a well-constructed stockade, while directly opposite it, within the stockade, was a large house divided into four for the use of the men. Another building stood on the right, while on the left was the trading store, and on the opposite side, across the square in the centre of the stockade, was a row of houses occupied in 1852 by the white miners.

"There were bastions at two opposite corners of the stockade; square at the bottom and octagonal at the top. In the lower part four guns were kept constantly ready for service, while the upper part of the bastions were loopholed for musketry."

A lot of time has passed since Mr. Hacking passed that way in the 28-foot *Elkay*, and it is possible that much change has occurred in that time. But Fort Rupert calls.

And so do the ghosts of the valiant Scandinavian settlements in the Cape Scott district at the tip of the Island; San Josef Bay, Newhitti, Shushartie, and Cape Scott.

There comes a call, also, from the ghosts of the fishing stations of Cachalot, near Kyuquot, Hecate on historic Nootka Island, and Sechart on Barkley Sound, from Roy on Loughborough Inlet amongst the maze of islands north of Campbell River, and from nearby Channeton.

Another sound is heard from the Queen Charlotte Island; from Sewell, Naden Harbour and Rose Harbour, to name but three.

Perhaps these summons will never be answered by us, but there they are, or there they were, and the adventurous, the romantic, the curious, or the dreamer—and yes, the idiot—will never get them out of his system until he has set foot within their confines, and thus stills the voice which calls all those who cannot resist the two-worded phrase "ghost town."

PART VII

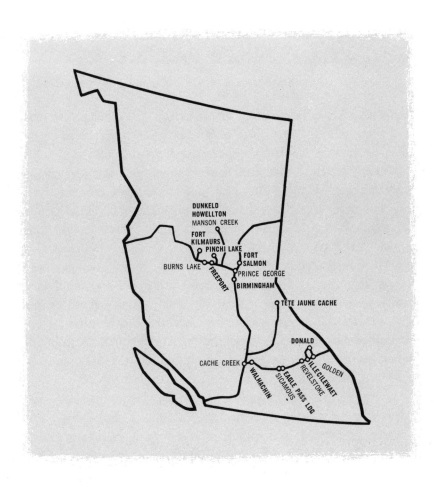

The tent city of Tete Jaune Cache during construction of the Grand Trunk Pacific Railway, now part of the Canadian National Railways System.

Tete Jaune Cache, Birmingham, Fort Fraser, East New Hazelton and Freeport

THIS ODYSSEY has only scratched the surface. Many other places remain, scattered about the province whose only record of existence is to be found on old maps, mining reports and ancient newspaper items.

Early in our search of adventure in ghost towns we boarded a combined passenger and way-freight at Red Pass Junction on the *Canadian National Railway* and headed for Tete Jaune Cache—British Columbia's Sodom and Gomorrah during the construction of the *Grand Trunk Pacific Railway* which now forms part of the *CNR*.

Tete Jaune's reputation was established early in its brief existence as the "largest tent city in British Columbia", and it persisted until the last tent was folded. At one time it tried to emerge from a tent city into a log city, but the provincial government accused the builders of taking Crown timber without paying a royalty on it. After that those buildings which had been erected were torn down, tossed into the river, and canvas took its place once more.

The town, named after a yellow-headed half-breed trader of the fur trade days who had a cache near the base of Mount Robson, was a typical "end of steel" village. It was important as a barging centre for construction supplies down-river as far west as Fort George, now Prince George.

J. A. Lower, writing in the July 1940 issue of the *British Columbia Historical Quarterly*, describes vividly such a village as "one of the phenomena of railroad building."

"The end of steel village," he wrote, "was built around the Pioneer, the mechanical track-layer—an ungainly overgrown box car with weird, semi-human arms. The village is always three miles from the end of steel. That is positively the only restraint it knows; for within that distance of the end of steel the contractor has complete legal control on unsettled areas. And knowing the hell that lives in those shacks, he pushes them to the extreme of his authority.

"An 'end of steel' village is made up of boots, billiards and belles. It is the home of the illicit liquor traffic of construction and the residence of women who never elsewhere enjoyed so much freedom. Three-quarters of the shacks are restaurants in front—for about six feet. The restaurant is merely an outward plausible excuse for the existence of the shack.

"Back of the little counter is the pool room, and then, through a small doorway, up a short flight of steps that breathes exclusiveness and privacy is the real object of existence—the card room.

"Free bunk houses are the provision of the contractors for the disabled, helpless bohunk who has spent the evening and everything else in the other shacks.

"At 50-Mile [50 miles from Lucerne on the B.C.-Alberta boundary] there was even a bath house, but it failed ignominiously but not unexpectedly.

"At Fitzhugh, which is within the province of Alberta, the lid was kept closed a little by the mounted police, but their jurisdiction ended at the border of British Columbia, and there at the summit, right on the boundary, the doors were wide open, and down through the Miles 17, 29 and 50 they remained that way. Mile 29 had a reputation of which its inhabitants refused to be proud.

"A special selection of shacks grew up at the western end of the pass on the site of the Tete Jaune Cache Indian village. An old Negress ran the town . . . an 'end of steel' village is a disgrace, but Tete Jaune was indescribable."

Tete Jaune has left us no Colonel Lowery to record the foibles of the town, and there are few newspaper references to it. Possibly everybody was so ashamed of the tent city they closed their eyes to it and hoped the world would forget. Tete Jaune's contribution to the visible is just a few rotting logs along the banks of the Fraser which probably at one time served as launching ramps for the many barges which were sent down river. Perhaps the fact that the logs are rotting is, in a sense, poetic justice.

Before and after Tete Jaune Cache's natal day the real estate promoters moved in, and along the right-of-way of the *G.T.P.* they dreamed great dreams. And, lo! how they could dream! Some were honest, while others had that touch of larceny in them that made people suspect the legitimate real estate man.

As early as 1910 the Birmingham Townsite Company Limited, with offices at 519 Granville in Vancouver, was touting Birmingham as being "destined to be the SECOND GREATEST CITY in British Columbia."

"Because Birmingham is situated (1) at the logical and geographical centre of British Columbia—the greatest and wealthiest province of the Dominion (2) on the mainline of the G.T.P Railway, equi-distant from the three great cities of Vancouver, Edmonton and Prince Rupert; (3) at the meeting point of six projected railways; (4) on the conjunction of the great Fraser and Nechacco rivers—1000 miles of navigable waterways."

Thus went a full-page advertisement in the Vancouver *Province* for March 12, 1910. And then came the clincher:

"Here's your chance to get in on the ground floor. We offer 1000 lots at $50 each—$25 cash—and guarantee absolutely that these lots will in two and a half months be selling at from $150 to $200. Don't delay."

There was also the Fort Salmon townsite, 20 miles north of Fort (Prince) George:

PLANT YOUR DOLLARS IN FORT SALMON
THE HOUR OF FRUITAGE IS AT HAND

And, there was East New Hazelton:

"Greatest Subscription Premium Ever Offered By A Magazine!" read an advertisement in the *Province* for July 8, 1914. "Nothing to Equal it has ever been attempted . . . The Canadian Magazine, Canada's acknowledged leading monthly is making this exceptional offer to you. Subscribe to The Canadian Magazine for two years at the regular price, and receive a lot 33 by 120 in East New Hazelton FREE (with the exception of a small fee to cover costs of survey, delivery of deed, etc.) . . . Lots in this very neighbourhood are selling from $150 to $1,500 and prices are increasing rapidly. Grasp this unique opportunity now. There are no strings to this offer, the reputation of The Canadian Magazine is your

Smuggled whisky, seized by the police in Tete Jaune Cache.

ample guarantee that every statement made here is genuinely true."

The advertisement concluded that "The Canadian Magazine is in the publishing business and not in the real estate business."

There were others: Willow City, Central Fort George, Kitamaat, Canyon City, and many more. Most, like Birmingham and Fort Salmon, are still waiting for their first building, and they probably will wait for a long time to come.

All these, in a way, were "ghosts" or perhaps "phantoms"? They began in the same way as many of the others visited on this odyssey, but they never had anything behind them more substantial than hot air.

The case of Freeport, a construction town east of present-day Burns Lake, is slightly different. At one time, it is reported, Freeport had 3000 residents, all workers on the *Grand Trunk Pacific* with the exception of the saloon keepers, those excelling in dealing from the bottom of the deck, and the chatelaines of little cottages with red curtains on the windows. Now all that remains is a solitary grave, set in a lovely grove of poplar trees on a hill overlooking the site of the former town. The grave is that of Denver Ed Kelly, a husky former pugilist who was playing poker in the back room of a "cigar store" on the night of July 29, 1913. Across the table was Jerry Mulvinhill, Irish as County Down, who on the night in question was packing a gun.

After the pot had been built up to a considerable size, Mulvinhill "called" and Denver Ed laid down his hand. It contained four lovely aces, and Kelly reached out to draw in his winnings.

"Not so fast," said Mr. Mulvinhill, and he laid down his hand, which strangely enough, contained a single ace. Now in any game, five aces is generally considered unfair. It certainly was in the eyes of Mr. Mulvinhill. The other patrons of the cigar store suddenly remembered appointments elsewhere. Denver Ed and Jerry Mulvinhill were alone. There was one shot, and Kelly lay dead on the floor.

The law sentenced Mulvinhill to hang on the gallows, but at the last moment his sentence was commuted to life imprisonment. Legend says that after the railway construction men had passed to the westward, Kelly's sister bought the townsite and had it razed to leave only the grave of her brother, the man who held one too many aces.

Germansen Creek, Manson Creek, Dunkeld, Howellton, Old Hogem, New Hogem, Pinchi Lake and Fort Kilmaurs

OUT FROM Vanderhoof and north, beyond the old Hudson's Bay trading post of Fort St. James, stretches a good gravel road into the heartland of the vast Omineca country. The traveller up this road is riding with history, for in 1869 gold was discovered by Twelve-Foot Davis, formerly of Barkerville, on Arctic Creek and in the winter of 1869-70 Vital LaForce wintered on the headwaters of the Omineca River. Other creeks, Manson and Germansen, were found to be gold bearing, and the Omineca gold rush was on.

At the junction of Germansen and the Omineca the town of Germansen, sometimes called Arctic City or Omineca City, arose. Hubert Howe Bancroft, in his *History of British Columbia*, published in 1887, tells us that during the first winter it contained "eighteen inhabitants but by the summer of 1871 counted twenty substantial wooden buildings comparing favorably with those at Barkerville."

A writer to the *Cariboo Sentinel* at Barkerville, on August 12, 1871 said Omineca City was "a big town with nothing in it" and added that Joe Blum had started his whisky mill; "he deals it out on a board in one corner of an unfinished house."

214

Fifteen miles east, a former member of the company of Royal Engineers, Robert Howell, discovered the Manson Creek diggings and the towns of Manson, Dunkeld and Howellton arose.

"Saloons, cards, fur traders, miners and Hydah squaws for *genre;* ditch drains, log cabins and stick forests for scenery, these," Bancroft wrote, "made up what was regarded as the somewhat miserable picture of the town of Manson Creek."

One of the most important people in town was Rufus Sylvester, packer and miner extraordinary, who was to carve a name for himself in the northland which only the great Cataline could approach. Dancing Bill Latham was also there with his music box and terpsichorean jewels.

The *Colonist* noted on August 1871 that Dunkeld consisted of three buildings, including a "theatre with real actors." This remarkable enterprise consisted of a troupe of actors-turned-miners led by a Mr. and Mrs. McGinley and their daughters, who every fortnight put on a show which brought out the entire population of Manson, Howellton, and Dunkeld. Between rehearsals Mr. McGinley did a little gold washing under the theatre, and made at least $500 for his work. If he made any profits from the stage it is not reported, but it is to be hoped he made more from the thespian arts than from mining.

At the same time, Howellton consisted of "two stores and four other buildings."

To the westward, on the Omineca River, was Old Hogem, one of the small communities which never grew up, but owed its being to the resourcefulness of a legendary trader from Iowa. This particular gentleman was unlucky in the mines, so he opened a store with practically no stock, and waited. In due course he spread a rumour of a new strike on another creek, and bought up all the supplies the miners had on hand as they set out for the new diggings. Later, when they found they had been humbugged, our Iowan merchant sold them back their own provisions and tools at double the price, sometimes even triple, what he had paid for them. Thus, he earned the name of Old Hog'em. The following year, an opposition store was started nine miles below, and this man charged even higher prices than Old Hog'em, and his place was dubbed New Hogem.

These are the ghosts of the Omineca, which, unfortunately, this odyssey was unable to visit. It is reported, however, that much of interest will be found up this lonely road, including the ghost town of Pinchi Lake where, during the Second World War, the Consolidated Mining & Smelting

Company operated the largest mercury mine in the world. It produced 1200 tons of the mineral each month, but with the end of hostilities the demand for mercury dropped and the mine ceased operation. A post office was established at Pinchi Lake on April 1, 1942, closing down with the mine on August 30, 1947.

In the days of the fur trade this great mountainous area was known as New Caledonia, a name given to it by the explorer Simon Fraser. It was dotted with little fur trading establishments, outpost of Fort St. James, "the fur capital." One of these was Fort Kilmaurs, sometimes known as Fort Babine, and latterly as Old Fort. It was built on the shore of Babine Lake in 1822 by Chief Trader William Brown and was named after a parish in his native Ayrshire, Scotland. The post was moved to the westward to the present site of Babine in 1836, but for years afterwards the settlement continued to flourish as a little outpost of civilization tucked away in an almost forgotten corner of the province.

An account in the *Northern Sentinel* of Kitimat, published on May 11, 1961, stirred our ghost-town feelings and Old Fort's name is high on the list of places we would like to visit.

Writing in that newspaper, Manny Martin had this to say of Old Fort:

"We pulled into shore and were promptly greeted by a friendly aroma of rotting moose-meat . . . The setting for the village was without doubt carefully chosen, probably by a people who lived there many hundreds of years before the white man came. The site contains a really breathtaking view of the large expanse of lake to the south, as well as the entrances of both the northern arms of the lake.

"At the present time, there are still several dozen houses, as well as a huge church which sits on the side of a hill overlooking the whole village. We walked around feeling rather awed by it all. Here Indians of by-gone days had lived and died.

"We walked by the graveyard now overgrown with weeds and shrubs, saw rosaries placed there by a grieving wife or husband or parent, around the top of the gravestones.

"We visited the old church, which had taken many people many hours to build. Everything was still there, and one had only to close his eyes to envisage the priest of former days ministering to his flock.

"It all gave us a feeling of the past which can never be gleaned from books. Here was history!—and we were walking in the midst of it."

General view of Walhachin in 1911, with luxurious hotel in background.

Walhachin, Eagle Pass Landing, Illecillewaet and Donald

THE GHOSTS of Walhachin are not the ghosts of a town but of a fantastic drama which unfolded on these broad, sage brush covered benchlands of the Thompson about 14 miles east of Cache Creek in the years between 1907 and 1914. Its ghosts are the shrivelled remains of orchards, of bone-dry, smashed flumes, which once brought water to the fruitlands, and possibly, you can say, of a way of life that went out with the cannonading of the First World War.

It began in 1907 when an American engineer, C. E. Barnes, saw the possibility of irrigating the dry benches above the Thompson River to create a paradise where the little *CPR* station of Penny's was located. He interested an English nobleman, the Marquis of Anglesey, in the project, and with his backing the British Columbia Horticultural Estate was formed.

A large area of Crown Land was purchased at a dollar an acre, the

217

Penny Ranch was absorbed and a dam was built on Deadman Lake. Miles of ditch and trestlework were constructed to bring the precious water over deep ravines and up and down steep slopes to the fledgling orchards. By 1911, 3000 acres were irrigated, and half of this was under cultivation.

An elaborate brochure was issued to attract settlers. The introduction said, "Fruit growing in your Province has acquired the distinction of being a beautiful art as well as a most profitable industry . . . No expense has been spared to make the system of irrigation one of the finest in the Province . . ."

Many retired Imperial Army officers and men arrived to take up the "beautiful art" and settle on the 50-acre townsite, with its modern hotel, school, community hall and general store. About 40 homes were built, some of stone, with high-ceilinged living rooms, dens, and great fire places in which cord-sized timbers burned merrily on the long, cold winter nights.

The orchards of Walhachin, 1911. The photograph was taken from a publicity brochure.

The orchards of Walhachin, 1961.

The hotel was magnificent, with three rotundas, spacious public rooms and fine accommodations. But, if any man dared enter the public or dining rooms in work clothes or shirt sleeves, an immaculately dressed steward would gently, but firmly, suggest the wrong-doer leave and come back in proper attire, in other words, dressed as a gentleman. Or, he could stay in the kitchen.

Walhachin was no place for the idler, or the man who refused to allow dirt to get under his finger nails. The work was exasperatingly hard, and it was not until four years after the first tree was planted that the experiment showed signs of success. Where other towns might have had saloons, Walhachin had Class, and no member of the community, no matter how hard he toiled in the fields, was ever permitted to forget it. There were servants and valets, maids and a Chinese laundry. There was a swimming pool, a skating rink, polo, and a community hall with a wonderful dance floor. There were piano recitals, played on the grand

219

piano used by the great Polish pianist Paderweski during his 1910 American tour.

And then came the war.

Cablegrams from Britain, recalling the men to their regiments, began to arrive. Every man expected his call at any moment, and after the day's work was finished, he went to drill on an improvised parade-ground. Soon the orchards were woefully short of man-power, and the burden fell on the older men and those too young for military service.

While the men were at the front, disaster struck the "Garden of Eden" by the Thompson. A heavy rainstorm took out the flumes, cutting off the life-giving supply of water. It was a hopeless situation. The men were too few in number to repair the damage, the sap in the apple trees began to dry up under the intense summer heat, and the sage brush and tumble weed returned.

After the war, many of the men who had laboured so hard and so successfully at Walhachin remained in England. They despaired of having

The gracious homes of Walhachin, 1961.

to start afresh. Some returned, but the Marquis of Anglesey, who had put $1,500,000 into the project, called it quits. He offered the land to the provincial government as a soldier settlement scheme, but it was refused. Instead a project was started in the South Okanagan around Oliver.

For a few years, Walhachin lingered on, but a change had come. Dress was no longer required in the hotel dining room, homes became empty and began to sag. Discouragement set in, and with the raising of the freight rates on fruit in the early 1930s, Walhachin's days were over.

Today it is a peaceful little community composed mostly of old age pensioners. The hotel has gone, the grand piano is at the University of British Columbia, and, with the exception of some fields down by the Thompson, the orchards are dead.

A highway marker alongside the Trans-Canada Highway tells the story in eleven lines, concluding with, "Now only the ghosts of flume, trees and homes remain to mock this once thriving settlement."

It is rather interesting to note, that in the middle 1860s, great flocks of men passed this way enroute to the Big Bend gold fields north of Revelstoke. Now another rush is taking place. Tourists have found it a quick and easy way to reach the playgrounds of the Rockies, through Rogers Pass, east of Revelstoke. And as they drive eastward, through a scenic wonderland, they will pass several ghosts of the past, probably without realizing it.

Our goal now was Donald Station, at the far end of Rogers Pass, and enroute we stopped at Sicamous to see whether some vestige of old Eagle Pass Landing could be found.

Eagle Pass Landing was a place of some importance in the construction of the last link of the *Canadian Pacific Railway*. It was only 16 miles from Craigellachie, where on November 7, 1885 the last spike of the railway was driven. With that ceremony, Eagle Pass Landing went out of business after less than a year of life. From Savona, at the head of Kamloops Lake, right up to the Landing, a small fleet of steamers hauled supplies to the way-camps along the Thomson River and Shuswap Lake. In life it wasn't very much, just a cluster of shacks on the lake front, but in death, it paved the way for the founding of Sicamous.

At the site we found an old root house which may or may not have been a survivor of the old Landing, and we found more mosquitoes per square inch than we had ever endured. We felt sorry for the railway

Eagle Pass Landing, 1885.

construction men who had to stay there under those circumstances.

On this, our second visit to Revelstoke during our travels, the town was much too busy to talk about that dam business. The main topic was Rogers Pass, recently opened as a link in the Trans-Canada Highway, and we joined the throng for the scenic drive through the Selkirk Mountains, following a river with one of the most beautiful names in British Columbia, the Illecillewaet.

At one time there was a town by that name, situated about 14 miles east of Revelstoke. Now even the railway station is closed and the lovely, lyrical name is removed from the time tables.

It first appeared in 1885 and a year later the Lanark mine at nearby Laurie was staked by T. W. Bain. Illecillewaet was a noisy place, wide open to all the temptations to which the flesh is heir. The moralist will say it deserved its fate, for Illecillewaet was swept up by an avalanche.

One who visited Illecillewaet was William Spotswood Green who set down his impressions in a book entitled *Among the Selkirk Glaciers*, published in 1890.

The town he said was a "typical frontier village, the inhabitants being prospectors, miners engaged in the silver mines high up in the mountains to the northward, lumbermen and those associated with the *Canadian Pacific Railway*. Burnt black trunks alternated with wooden houses, some of which stood on legs in swampy pools only half-reclaimed from the overflow of the river by piles of empty meat tins, broken packing cases, etc., which were littered everywhere."

Not much of a tribute to a town, it is true, but in the annals of the mining industry in B.C., Illecillewaet rates higher, for this town was the transfer point for the first regular shipments by rail of silver-lead ore for a smelter from any mining operation in the province.

Beyond the pass lay little Donald, a former divisional point on the *C.P.R.* and now a small sawmilling community with little or no evidence of its past stature. Donald had its supply of sinners, but more important, it had a saint in the person of the Rev. Henry Irwin, better known as Father Pat, the beloved Anglican priest of railway construction and Rossland mining camp days. He was not a brilliant preacher, but he was a Samaritan, ever at the service of others, particularly when tragedy struck the little railway community, as it frequently did.

On the opposite side of the fence were such people as One Armed Roxy, and there was a real artist for you. He could shuffle the cards with one hand and then deal them off the bottom of the deck so slickly that even a sharp-eyed man watching him couldn't detect the trick. Roxy plied his craft up and down the mainline, with particular emphasis on Field, Donald and Revelstoke where the pickings were best. Another of his fraternity was 20-year-old Keno Jack, a Pennsylvania-Dutchman whose proper name was John Houts. His legitimate profession was that of carpenter, and the old timers speak highly of his skill in the field, but when it came to cards, he was said to be utterly devoid of principles.

One night in Donald, Keno was shot at close range across a draw poker table by a *CPR* conductor named Jack Selkirk and was badly wounded in the lung. Selkirk had caught him in the act of springing a cold deck, and Keno would have died if it had not been for the ministrations of Florence Mackenzie, the notorious Mother Mackenzie. Selkirk hit for the border after the shooting and was never heard from again.

St. Peter's Church, Windermere.

St. Paul's Church, Golden.

Keeping a watchful eye on Donald's malefactors was Stephen Redgrave, sheriff of Kootenay, who made arrests that none but a *coeur de lion* would have made. In off duty hours he would sit before the pot-bellied stove in the sheriff's office and tell the most atrocious lies *a la* Baron Munchausen, thus earning the title of "the most aristocratic liar in the Kootenay."

Little things like one-arm card sharps, illicit whisky, soiled doves and drunks were nothing in comparison with Donald's great robbery, committed by one of the leading citizens. Rufus Kimpton, staunch supporter of the church, stole Father Pat's church—lock, stock and barrel!

When, in the winter of 1897, the *CPR* decided to abandon Donald in favor of Revelstoke, the company offered to transport any and all buildings in the town, free of charge, to any point along their line. Everything went, and Donald vanished from the face of the earth. Kimpton, who was going south to Windermere, decided to take the church with him and in so doing he got the people of Revelstoke fighting-mad. Apparently the bishop had promised them the church, but when a work crew of Revelstokians arrived in Donald they found, lo and behold, the church had vanished.

As soon as it was discovered Windermere had the little church, an exchange of rather unecclesiastical letters ensued in which Revelstoke demanded the return of their "stolen church." Windermere took the stand that possession was nine points of the law and ignored the correspondence. But then they found that Golden had played a cowardly trick on them. While the church was enroute to its new location, the people of Golden helped themselves to the church bell. Golden thereupon used the same arguments Windermere had used in dealing with Revelstoke, and now that the shoe was on the other foot, Windermere didn't like it a bit. The rivalry between the two simmered for more than 50 years, and then, in 1957, under cover of night, a party from Windermere descended upon Golden and stole the bell back again. A great victory parade was held in Windermere to celebrate the occasion, but in higher church circles the act was frowned upon, and the bell was returned to Golden.

And so, to see the ghosts of Donald we drove into Golden to visit the little Anglican church of St. Paul's, sometimes called St. Paul's of the Stolen Bell, and then south to Windermere to St. Peter's, the famed "Stolen Church".

Here, by this little white-steepled church, we regretfully brought our Odyssey of the Ghost Towns to an end.

Acknowledgements

To PARAPHRASE COLONEL Lowery's "Subscribers are the nicest people!", let us say here at the end of this Odyssey, that the many friends, new and old, whom we met along the way were "the nicest people", too.

To all of them, we say "thank you"—especially the old timers who gave us so generously of their time and knowledge, and to the museums and historical societies throughout the province which are doing so much to preserve the history of their areas.

We would also like to thank Mr. and Mrs. Andy Daney of Ferguson, Mr. and Mrs. Tom Reed of Trout Lake City, Mr. and Mrs. Ed Cook, of Princeton, Mr. and Mrs. Craigie Hood of Cassiar, Mr. J. C. Berry of the Cassiar Asbestos Corp. mine, Captain and Mrs. Douglas Whiffen of Whitehorse, Y. T., and Mr. Roy Minter of the *White Pass & Yukon Route*. Also Miss Nancy Miles of Cranbrook, Mrs. Harold White of Fernie, Mr. Randy Sandner of Cascade, Captain Norman Evans-Atkinson of Likely, Mr. and Mrs. Fred Ludditt of Wells, the late Mr. Fred Tregillus of Barkerville, Mr. Billy Clark of Howser, Mr. Archie Oakie of Camborne, and Mr. Rich. Hobson of El Carrito, California.

Very special thanks go, also, to the Leon and Thea Koerner Foundation for their generous assistance, and to Mr. Willard E. Ireland and his staff at the Provincial Library in Victoria. The help of Mr. Ron D'Altroy of the Vancouver Public Library's Northwest History room is also acknowledged with gratitude as is that of the Rover Motor Company of North America, who kindly put a Land-Rover at our disposal. My thanks also to Mr. Pierre Berton for permission to quote from his excellent history of the gold rush of '98, *The Klondike Fever*, and to Mr. Norman Hacking for his valued advice.

To Mr. W. E. Topping of Vancouver goes my appreciation for acting as photographer in the Lardeau, Slocan and Barkerville, and to Mr. Al. Hooker, who photographed Port Douglas, Quesnelle Forks and the Bullion for us.

To my wife, Betty, and the children, Douglas and Jane, go thanks which words cannot express, for their help in the field, and in the long hours at home, while this book was under preparation.